AN ATLAS OF WORLD HISTORY

AN ATLAS
OF
WORLD HISTORY

Dr S. de VRIES

Prof. T. LUYKX

W. O. HENDERSON, M.A. Ph.D

NELSON
1965

Thomas Nelson and Sons Ltd

36 Park Street London W1
Parkside Works Edinburgh 9
117 Latrobe Street Melbourne C1
10 Warehouse Road Apapa Lagos

Thomas Nelson and Sons (Africa) (Pty) Ltd
P.O. Box 9881 Johannesburg

Thomas Nelson and Sons (Canada) Ltd
81 Curlew Drive Don Mills Ontario

Thomas Nelson and Sons
Copewood and Davis Streets Camden 3, N.J.

Originally published as ELSEVIERS HISTORISCHE ATLAS
(Amsterdam-Elsevier)

CONTENTS

BLACK-AND-WHITE SKETCH MAPS

Introduction to World History

ANTIQUITY

The Eastern nations until the fall of the Persian Empire

The oldest civilisations are found in river valleys: in China, India, and the 'Fertile Crescent', which consists of the regions watered by the Nile, the Jordan, the Euphrates, and the Tigris. It is these valley civilisations of the Near East that form the source of the culture of the modern world.

Egypt. The annual overflowing of the Nile gave Egypt its fertility. It occurred with such regularity, generally on 19 July, that it formed the basis of the system whereby time was computed, that is, of the calendar (possibly from 4241 B.C. onwards). Irrigation activities along the Nile demanded a powerful central authority, and consequently, when the various small states were combined to form a single kingdom (before 3000 B.C.), the king (Pharaoh) possessed absolute power and was worshipped as a god. ❥ Life in Egypt was entirely ruled by religion, and particularly by the belief that the vital force (*ka*) continues as long as the body exists. This led to the preservation of the bodies of the dead and to the construction of huge tombs for the Pharaohs – first the pyramids and later rock-tombs such as that of Tutankhamen (c. 1325 B.C.), which was discovered in this century. Prominent people were buried in *mastabas*. Entire towns of the dead arose on the west bank of the Nile opposite Memphis and Thebes, and it is sepulchral art and temples that most clearly reveal the monumental character of Egyptian civilisation. The walls of the tomb-chamber were covered with reliefs, paintings, etc., depicting the deceased's life as accurately as possible, while portraits on the mummy-case and elsewhere made it possible for the *ka* to visit him. The use of natural stone, the dry climate, and the isolated position of Egypt are the main reasons why the discovery of tombs and numerous papyri has resulted in detailed knowledge of life in ancient Egypt. The Egyptians were polytheistic and worshipped the sun-god Ra and the god of the dead, Osiris, as well as other gods and numerous animals. An attempt by the Pharaoh Akhenaton in the fourteenth century B.C. to put some life into their formalised religion failed. He introduced a monotheistic sun-worship at his new capital Tell el-Amarna. But when he died the people reverted to their old beliefs. ❥ Their script was pictorial and alphabetic. It was deciphered by the Frenchman Champollion at the beginning of the nineteenth century A.D. with the aid of the Rosetta Stone, which bore the same text in hieroglyphics and Demotic Egyptian and Greek. The country was conquered by the Persians in 525 B.C.; despite this, however, it enjoyed a high degree of prosperity until Roman times.

Mesopotamia has preserved fewer traces of its civilisation than Egypt. It was more exposed to invaders than Egypt, and, at any rate in the south, the chief building material used was not stone but clay. One of the oldest city-states was Ur of the Chaldees, from which Abraham emigrated. ❥ After various invasions by Semitic peoples the Babylonian Empire was created. The legislation of one Babylonian ruler, Hammurabi (c. 1700 B.C.), has survived; it shows a close resemblance to Jewish law. ❥ At a

PLATES, *from top to bottom:* The sphinx at Giza, Old Kingdom (c. 2460 B.C.). – Bust of Theban official of the New Kingdom. – Coloured relief from the tomb of Horemheb. – Assyrian relief showing a chariot (eighth century B.C.).

9

later date the Assyrian Empire gained supremacy (1200–612 B.C.). Its kings left a permanent record of their martial exploits and hunting expeditions on stone reliefs in their huge palace-fortresses. One of the greatest Assyrian kings was Ashurbanipal (seventh century B.C.), who conquered not only Egypt but also large areas of Asia Minor. The Assyrians, who were hated for their inhumanity, were defeated by the Medes and Babylonians, and their capital Nineveh was destroyed (612 B.C.). Babylon experienced another period of prosperity under Nebuchadnezzar. Jerusalem was taken and the Jews were led off into the 'Babylonian Captivity' (587 B.C.). This lasted until 539 B.C., when Babylon fell to the Persians. ͽ The 'Tower of Babel' was one of the many temple-towers or ziggurats from whose tops the priests studied the stars. It is to these men that we owe the division of our week into seven days and the division of the day into hours, minutes, and seconds. ͽ Whole libraries have been found containing clay tablets covered with cuneiform writing, a modified pictographic script.

The Hittites. Only in recent times has much been learned about the third great independent civilisation of Asia Minor, that of the Hittites. Their great empire grew outwards from Anatolia and attained its zenith about 1800 B.C. It collapsed c. 1200 B.C. as a result of the Indo-European migrations, which caused upheavals throughout Asia Minor and Greece. Their civilisation was related to that of Mesopotamia but more primitive. Their laws, however, were much more humane, as was their treatment of defeated enemies. ͽ Their language was related to the Indo-Germanic tongues such as Latin.

Phoenicia and Palestine. West of the Lebanon lived the Phoenicians, famous for their trade in purple dye and glass. They were the first nation to progress from a pictographic to an alphabetic script; they devised characters for 22 consonants – the source of our modern alphabet. ͽ The Jews inhabited Palestine, where they had settled under Abraham's leadership (c. 1800 B.C.). Recurrent famines compelled them to spend some time in Egypt, but Moses led them back to the Promised Land (c. 1300 B.C.), which fell to them after hard fighting. The Philistines on the coast, however, cut them off from the sea. The Jewish state was established under the Judges and later under the Kings Saul, David, and Solomon; Solomon also built the great Temple at Jerusalem. The kingdoms of Israel and Judah were set up in 930 B.C.; both succumbed to the ambitions of the Mesopotamian kings. Not until 539 B.C. were the Jews permitted by Cyrus to return and rebuild the Temple which Nebuchadnezzar had destroyed; and now it was as subjects of Persia. ͽ The Jews stubbornly and successfully defended their religion time and again, as for instance under Judas Maccabaeus (c. 160 B.C.). Jerusalem was taken by the Romans in A.D. 70. The Temple was again destroyed and the Jews were scattered over the world.

Persia. The Persians were the first Indo-European race to play a role in history. Living on the Iranian plateau, they originally led a very poor existence as peasants, until their king Cyrus (c. 550 B.C.) conquered Lydia and the rest of the Asia Minor coast which had been colonised by the Greeks, as well as Babylonia and Palestine. His son Cambyses conquered Egypt in 525 B.C.; but his successors, Darius I and Xerxes, failed in their attempts to subjugate Greece. ͽ The Persians' contribution to culture lies in the fact that they were the first nation in history to create and

PLATES, *from top to bottom:* Hittite soldiers in a chariot during an attack. – Tombs hewn in the rocks at Petra. – Mythical monster from the palace of Darius at Persepolis. – Another fragment from this palace, showing men bringing tribute.

10

administer an empire. Their dualistic religion was an extremely moral one: in the struggle between the god of good and the god of evil men had to support the god of good, Ahura-Mazda, by leading a good and upright life. How highly developed their ethics were can be seen from the fact that some centuries later a new monotheistic religion, Mithraism, long vied for supremacy with Christianity. The excessive independence which the satraps (provincial governors) had acquired by about 300 B.C. enabled Alexander the Great of Macedon to conquer the Persian Empire quickly.

⁋ The civilisations so far dealt with have common features: there is frequently a divine priest-kingship, and, except among the Jews, there is a total absence of democracy. The concept of citizenship is completely unknown. Culturally, however, the states of the Near East were of the greatest significance for Greek and Roman civilisation.

Greece

Greek civilisation is the basis of Western European culture. Although the Greeks never managed to attain national political union, they developed the concepts of democracy and colonisation, while European art, literature, and philosophy would be inconceivable without the Greeks.

The earliest times. Of all European countries Greece lies closest to Asia. It thus came into contact at an early date with the civilisations which flourished there, for the country's numerous bays and islands had early on in their history encouraged the Greeks to take to the sea. Thus there arose in Crete a civilisation which owed much to the Asiatic cultures. Cretan civilisation flourished between 3000 and 1400 B.C., as can be deduced from the various palaces which have survived. It coincided with the Mycenaean culture on the mainland of Greece, in the Peloponnesus, although this was cruder than that of Crete.

⁋ Troy, which was destroyed c. 1200 B.C. and excavated in the last century by Schliemann, was one of the sites of this civilisation. About 1200 B.C., during the Dorian migrations, tribes from the north invaded Greece and laid it waste. ⁋ But on the ruins of the old civilisation there arose, from the intermarriage of the various national groups, a new culture called the Hellenic. The result was not, as in the East, a single state. Instead, city-states were formed; such a state the Greeks called a *polis*. The form of government might be aristocratic or democratic, but the states were never ruled by a king to whom divine honour had to be paid, as in the Near East. Yet their language, their religion, and their tradition made the Greeks feel that they formed a single people. The Delphic oracle and the Olympic Games united all Greeks, and even those who left Greece to found colonies on the coasts of the Mediterranean or the Black Sea retained a feeling of unity with their mother-country. In fact southern Italy (Magna Graecia) and Ionia became centres of Greek civilisation.

The great age of Greece. Ionia, which had been conquered by Persia, was the cause which led to a violent struggle between the Greeks and the Persians. The Greeks emerged victorious from the three Persian Wars, thanks mainly to the Spartan army and the Athenian fleet. The Athenians won the sea battle of Salamis in 480 B.C., and several years later the Delian or Attic Confederation was founded for the purpose of liberating Ionia. It was natural that Athens should take the lead in the movement; but this had internal consequences also.

⁋ The sailors of the fleet provided by the people of Athens had now to be

PLATES, *from top to bottom:* Altar of Mithras (Roman period). – The 'Throne of Minos' in the palace at Cnossus in Crete. – Ruins of the royal tombs at Mycenae. – The round temple (*tholos*) dedicated to the goddess Athena at Delphi.

11

given greater political rights. Athens developed into a very democratic commercial and industrial state relying on its sea power. The man who could lead the popular assembly led the state. ◗ This man was Pericles, the great statesman of Athens during the Golden Age (c. 460–430 B.C.). On the Acropolis, which the Persians had laid waste, he had built the magnificent temples and sculptures with which the name of Phidias will always be associated. He promoted the arts and sciences, and politically Athens seemed to be the centre of a great empire embracing the islands and coasts of the Aegean Sea. But its prosperity excited the envy of Sparta and Corinth, and it was defeated in the Peloponnesian War (431–404 B.C.), in the course of which Pericles died during an outbreak of plague.

Alexander the Great. The post-war distress in Greece was great, and many Greeks emigrated or became mercenaries abroad. There was a succession of internal wars, Persia once more took possession of Ionia, and Thebes dethroned Sparta as a military power by its use of the 'oblique phalanx', later improved upon by the Macedonians. The Macedonian king, Philip, finally defeated the Greeks at Chaeronea in 338 B.C., and this defeat meant the end of Greek independence: the stubborn individualism of the city-states had at last to be paid for. ◗ To win the favour of the Greeks the King promised to undertake an expedition to liberate Ionia, but he was assassinated before the plan could be carried out. The task fell to his son Alexander. This prince of genius, whose tutor had been the Greek philosopher Aristotle, regarded himself as the vehicle of Greek civilisation. He took Ionia without much trouble, and, profiting by Persian weakness, proceeded along the coast to Egypt. There the priests proclaimed him a god, an act which increased the respect in which he was held in the East but alienated his Greeks and Macedonians. At the only navigable outlet of the Nile he founded Alexandria, and then he moved by way of Mesopotamia to India, whence his soldiers finally forced him to turn back. He died in Babylon in 323 B.C. His empire disintegrated, for his generals, the 'Diadochi', severally seized Syria, Egypt, and Macedon, and smaller units such as Pergamum. But a new civilisation, the Hellenistic, embracing all these territories, arose from the mingling of Eastern and Western elements. Greek became the lingua franca throughout the eastern Mediterranean, but Eastern concepts of state and religion found their way to the West. Thus the Hellenistic civilisations came to exert a great influence on that of Rome and on Christianity.

Rome

The Romans, more practical by nature than the Greeks, made a different contribution to Western civilisation. It is true that they passed the Greek Hellenistic culture on to Western Europe; but they also added elements of their own to it: state organisation, Roman law, and civil engineering.

The time of the kings and the Republic. The Romans were strongly influenced not only by the Greeks but also by the Etruscans, who came probably from Asia Minor and in the seventh and sixth centuries B.C. established an empire in central Italy based on the region of Tuscany, which takes its name from them. Their language has still not been deciphered, but they have left behind magnificent monuments to their civilisation in their cemeteries. The variety of ways in which the Etruscans influenced the Romans can be seen in, for example, various elements of

PLATES, *from top to bottom:* Part of the 'Lion Terrace' at Delos. – Painting of a Greek warrior on an Attic amphora. – Greek fortifications: part of a fortress in the Peloponnesus. – Monument to those who fell at Chaeronea.

the Roman religion, the gladiatorial games, institutions such as the triumphal procession, and architectural features such as the arch, which enabled Roman builders to achieve far more than the Greeks. ❧ Rome itself, founded according to tradition in 754 B.C. by Romulus and Remus, descendants of the Trojan hero Aeneas, was in early days a town in the Etruscan empire. Seven kings are said to have reigned over it in succession, and when the last was expelled (510 B.C.) the period of Etruscan dominion ended. Rome now became an aristocratic republic whose system of government strongly resembled that of Sparta. The leading class was formed by patricians who governed the city through the Senate; the common people (the plebeians) had little influence. ❧ Until about 275 B.C. the conquest of Italy by the Romans was accompanied at home by increasingly successful attempts by the plebeians to obtain equality with the patricians. The various peoples of Italy, such as the Etruscans and Samnites, were subjected one after the other; the last to succumb were the Greeks in southern Italy (275 B.C.). The Romans allowed the defeated Italians a considerable measure of self-government, thus converting them rapidly from subjects into faithful allies. Italy was soon covered by a network of roads which made rapid troop movements possible. Meanwhile the plebeians were successfully acquiring greater rights. For example, the tribunes of the people were instituted; these, with their right of veto, were able to block decisions of the Senate which were unfavourable to the plebeians. Equality between the patricians and plebeians brought an end to class strife about the same time as Italy was conquered.

❧ Rome was consequently strong right from the start of the great struggle for power with Carthage, the powerful Phoenician colony which dominated the central Mediterranean basin. The might of Carthage was broken in the three Punic (i.e. Phoenician) Wars, although towards the end of the third century B.C. it looked as if the Carthaginian general Hannibal might crush Roman power (battle of Cannae, 216 B.C.). These wars brought Rome considerable territorial gains. By the time Carthage was razed in 148 B.C. the Romans had won Sicily, Sardinia, Corsica, Spain, and the western half of the North African coast from their adversaries. Greece, Macedonia, and Pergamum were added to these conquests in the second century B.C., so that the entire Mediterranean basin, with the exception of Syria and Egypt (both Roman in the first century B.C.), was in Roman hands. ❧ But Hannibal's campaigns in Italy had resulted in many peasants fleeing to Rome. There they led a poverty-stricken existence as proletarians, while wealthy Romans bought large estates in Italy at low prices and farmed them largely with slave labour. The chief product of these farms was cattle, because Sicily provided cheap supplies of grain. This situation resulted in the decline of the free peasant class in Italy. Social disturbances ensued to which the brothers Gaius and Tiberius Gracchus in vain tried to put an end (133 and 121 B.C.). The demagogue Marius absorbed many proletarians in the army about 100 B.C. in order to reduce unemployment. Although he had several successes with this army against invading Germanic tribes, the Roman forces had become an instrument in the hands of ambitious generals and statesmen. ❧ A struggle between supporters of the Senate, the aristocrats, and the people's party ended in the victory of the latter, led by Julius Caesar, who in the course of conquering Gaul (modern France and Belgium) had formed a well-disciplined army (58–51 B.C.). In his few years of sole rule he did much that was good, and his murder in 44 B.C. could not delay monarchy. (Once Octavian, Julius Caesar's great-nephew, had got rid of Mark Antony and his ally Cleopatra, Queen of Egypt, in 31 B.C., he accepted sovereign

PLATES, *from top to bottom:* Etruscan fresco at Tarquinii. – Bust of Hannibal. – Roman warship with prow and oars, manned by legionaries. – Terracotta relief showing games in the circus.

power as *princeps*, i.e. first citizen of the state.) Julius Caesar made two landings upon the English coast in 55 and 54 B.C.; and in A.D. 43 the Emperor Claudius made Britain part of the Roman Empire.

The Empire, during its first few centuries, meant a period of peace for the countries of Western Europe, during which Roman-Hellenistic civilisation took root in large parts of the Empire. Octavian (as Emperor usually known by his title Augustus, 'increaser of prosperity'), tried to extend his dominion to the natural frontiers formed by the Rhine, the Danube, the Sahara, and the Syrian Desert. An attempt to extend the frontier to the Elbe was shattered by the Roman defeat in the Teutoburgiensis Saltus (A.D. 9). Subsequent Emperors pursued a more or less defensive policy; the only exception was Trajan, who extended his frontiers by conquering Dacia (now Romania) c. 100. ◊ Under the Emperors Rome became more and more the centre of the then-known world, and the city itself was embellished by the construction of palaces and monuments. Yet signs of decline became obvious after A.D. 200. The Germanic tribes were threatening the frontiers along the Rhine and the Danube, and on the eastern frontier the Parthian Empire was a powerful source of danger just when Rome, under a succession of Emperors who were the creation of the army, was entering upon a century of civil war. Christianity, which was gaining ground, led many Romans to turn from the state and this world and build their hopes on the Kingdom of God, which, as Augustine, the Doctor of the Church, wrote, was not of this world. An end was finally put to the confusion by Diocletian (c. 300), who reorganised the entire Empire, concentrated all power in the Emperor, and proclaimed himself *Dominus et Deus* ('Lord and God'). The decline of Italy and Rome is obvious from Constantine the Great's decision in 330 to move his capital to Byzantium, thenceforth called Constantinople. The Christians, whom Diocletian had persecuted, were granted religious liberty under Constantine (Edict of Milan 313), and in the reign of Theodosius I Christianity became the state religion. On his death he divided the Empire between his two sons (395). The western half soon collapsed under the onslaughts of the barbarian invasions. The Teutonic tribes, pushed from behind by the Huns who had invaded Europe from Asia, swarmed over the frontiers of the Empire. Rome itself was several times ravaged (the first time in 410), and everywhere there arose Germanic states on former Roman territory: the Visigoths founded a kingdom in Spain and in France south of the Loire, the Franks established themselves in Belgium and northern France, the Vandals founded a piratical state in Africa with Carthage as its capital, and Angles and Saxons crossed over to Britain, which had been evacuated at the time of the abandonment of the Rhine frontier at the beginning of the fifth century. In 476 the last Emperor of the West, Romulus Augustulus, was dethroned by the Germanic leader Odoacer, who, however, sent the Imperial insignia to Constantinople, thus acknowledging the Eastern Roman Emperors' claim to the West.

PLATES, *from top to bottom:* Triumphal arch at Orange (first century B.C.). – Fragment from the base of Trajan's Column. – Barbarians submit to the Emperor Marcus Aurelius. – Fragment of an early Christian sarcophagus, representing the creation of man.

THE MIDDLE AGES

The early Middle Ages

Although the Christian Church, Latin, and various Roman traditions continued to exist, the decline of the Western Roman Empire was so marked that historians consider the year 500 as the start of a new era: the Middle Ages. The name dates back to about 1500, when a new interest in antiquity arose in Italy and people began to regard the period intervening as one of barbarism.

The Germanic kingdoms. With the exception of the Franks, the Germanic tribes proved unable to set up lasting states in the conquered territories. Odoacer's Italian kingdom was soon wrested from him by the Ostrogoth king Theodoric. Theodoric tried in vain to fuse the Germans and Romans, and after his death Italy was conquered by the Eastern Empire as the result of a protracted struggle (553). ⚓ The Visigoths, who had been driven from France by the Franks, were likewise unable to hold their own against the invading forces of Islam; the last Gothic king was killed in 711. ⚓ The Frankish kingdom, on the other hand, proved durable. King Clovis (the name is an older form of Louis) originally ruled over the area round Tournai; but when he died in 511 his kingdom comprised almost the whole of modern France and Belgium. His conversion to Christianity made possible the future fusion of Germans and Romans. He made Paris his capital, and his policy laid the foundation of a new nation and a new state, France.

The Eastern Roman Empire continued to exist, a mixture of Roman, Christian, and Eastern Hellenistic traditions. Its Roman character at first predominated, but the Eastern element rapidly grew in importance. Justinian (527–65) tried to restore the old Empire: he recovered North Africa, Italy, and southern Spain, while Roman law was codified in the famous *Corpus Juris*. The art of his time clearly showed Eastern elements, which are to be seen in the Church of Hagia Sophia in Constantinople and the mosaics at Ravenna. ⚓ After his death the strain proved to be too great. Except for several exarchates (Ravenna, Rome), Italy was lost to the Germanic Lombards who swept over the country. For the Bishop of Rome, the Pope, this meant increasing independence, since supervision of Rome from Constantinople was now virtually impossible. Gregory the Great (590–604) extended the papal authority considerably with the support of Frankish power, an arrangement from which both the Popes and the Frankish kings were to benefit (see p. 16). ⚓ The weakness of the Eastern Roman Empire was clearly revealed when Islam went over to the offensive. Nevertheless, the Empire managed to survive until 1453, fulfilling a twofold task: on the one hand it beat off Islam's attacks on Europe from Asia, and on the other it preserved classical civilisation until the time when Europe was once more able to profit by it.

Islam radically altered the political and religious situation in the area round the Mediterranean in the eighth century. Until the beginning of the seventh century the Arabs had practised a kind of polytheistic paganism; their religious centre was Mecca, to which the Black Stone, the Ka'aba ('cube'), attracted many pilgrims. Mohammed, however, who was familiar with Judaism and Christianity, brought monotheism to the

PLATES, *from top to bottom:* The Emperor Theodosius I at the circus in Constantinople. – Part of a Byzantine palace at Ravenna. – Brooch dating from the time of the Barbarian Invasions. – Interior of Hagia Sophia at Constantinople.

Arabs. His flight from Mecca to Medina, the Hejira, is the event from which the Mohammedan era is dated. His sayings, collected in the Koran after his death, preached his law by a combination of secular and spiritual authority. ⁋ Under Mohammed's successors, the Caliphs, Islam experienced a vast expansion: within a century large parts of the Byzantine Empire (Egypt, Syria, Palestine), as well as North Africa and Spain, fell into their hands. The last of these conquests took place under the Ommeyad dynasty. The Moorish leader Tariq landed in Spain at 'Tariq's Rock' (Jebel-Tariq, now Gibraltar), defeated the Visigoths, and within a few years conquered the entire Iberian peninsula. Only in the north did the Christians hold out, and it was from here that the reconquest of Spain, the *Reconquista*, later took place. This was not finally completed until 1492, when Granada fell. The Spanish nation with its characteristic fanaticism, bravery, and fidelity to its king was moulded in this religious struggle. ⁋ A Moorish invasion of France was repelled by Charles Martel at Poitiers in 732, while an attack on Constantinople in 717 had also failed. Europe was thus saved from Muslim domination. The power of Islam was also weakened by the fall of the Ommeyads in 750. One of them escaped to Spain and there founded his own kingdom which attained a high spiritual and material level (the Caliphate of Cordova or Western Caliphate). The Eastern Caliphate also experienced a period of great prosperity, particularly under Harun el-Rashid, a contemporary of Charlemagne; the Caliph himself is immortalised in the tales of the Arabian Nights. In many respects the Mohammedans were the inheritors of Hellenistic culture (mathematics, astronomy, medicine), so that Islamic civilisation was much in advance of that of Western and Central Europe.

Charlemagne. After Clovis's death (511) and the partition of his kingdom among his sons there followed a period of wars among titular Frankish kings who virtually left government to their Mayors of the Palace. It was one of the latter, Charles Martel ('the Hammer'), who repulsed the Moors at Poitiers. Charles and his son, Pepin the Short, vigorously supported the spread of Christianity by the agency of, for example, Willibald and Boniface and the monks who lived by the rule which Benedict of Nursia had established at Monte Cassino in 529. They also contributed actively to the spread of practical civilisation. The ties between the Church and the Carolingians were strengthened when the Pope, in exchange for the support which Pepin had given him against the Lombards, had him anointed king (751). The territory wrested from the Lombards, the 'Patrimony of St Peter', became the nucleus of the later States of the Church. Pepin's son Charlemagne (768–814) maintained good relations between Church and state, and was crowned Emperor by Pope Leo XII in Rome in 800. The Western Roman Empire was restored, but at the same time the seed of future strife for power between the Emperor and the Pope was also sown. ⁋ Charlemagne did much to promote the culture and well-being of his peoples. At his palaces there were writing schools for the children of his nobles. The feudal system, brought into use by Charles Martel, was further extended by Charlemagne; but the centrifugal forces set up by the system proved fatal to the Empire under his successors.

The high Middle Ages

Europe threatened. After Charlemagne's death in 814 a period began during which Western civilisation was in peril. The Frankish kingdom, partitioned in accordance with Germanic tradition in 843 by the Treaty

PLATES, *from top to bottom:* Damascus, mosque of the Ommeyads. – Arabesque from the mosque at Jerusalem. – Chapel in Valkhof Park at Nijmegen. – Ivory cover to psalter of Charles the Bald, inlaid with precious stones.

16

of Verdun among the three sons of Charlemagne's son Louis le Débonnaire, was no longer an important power, so that the Normans and Saracens pressed hard on all sides in western and southern Europe. Mohammedans and Slavs assaulted the walls of Constantinople and Slav tribes pushed along the Elbe deep into Germany. The force of their attack did not diminish until the Hungarians from Asia established themselves on the Danube, thus splitting Slav territory into two parts. The relics of ancient civilisation survived only in the now restricted territories of the Eastern Empire. ❧ Yet some relieving features are discernible. The Treaties of Verdun and Meersen had laid the basis of France and Germany. In Eastern Europe the Normans figured as merchants and founders of states. On their expeditions along the Russian rivers to Constantinople they founded the kingdoms of Novgorod and Kiev which, converted to Christianity from Constantinople, were of such great importance for the Russia of the future. The Balkan Slavs also founded states after their conversion, and they, too, were subject to the influence of Byzantine culture.

The Holy Roman Empire had very soon after 843 acquired the buffer territory consisting of the Netherlands (except the Province of Flanders, which belonged to France), Lorraine, Switzerland, and northern Italy. On the death of the last Carolingian the German nobles chose a new king, Henry of Saxony (911), who immediately started driving back the Magyars and Slavs. His son and successor Otto I continued this policy, and his prestige became so great that the Pope crowned him Emperor (962). The weaknesses of the 'Holy Roman Empire' were, however, immediately manifest. In the first place, it was elective, and the nobles preferably chose weak Emperors; in the second place, the Emperors came in the long run to prefer their Italian to their German territories, which further increased the danger of disintegration. ❧ It is not surprising that in the eleventh century the nobles and the Pope (Gregory VII) combined against Henry IV, who was forced to submit to the humiliation of Canossa (1077). For his part Henry could count on the German cities because they needed a central authority, and on the bishops, in whose interest it was to have a weak Pope. This struggle for power between the Emperor and the Pope – each regarded himself as the heir of the Roman Emperors – had as one of its causes the question of who should control the nomination of bishops, and it is therefore sometimes called the Investiture Contest. Although a compromise was reached in 1122 the struggle continued. The powerful German princely house of Hohenstaufen was finally extinguished in the struggle against the Pope (1268). But the power of the Pope, too, was so weakened that he succumbed in a subsequent conflict against the French king.

England. In the ninth century the Norsemen began at first to raid and then to settle in England. Although they were defeated by Alfred, King of Wessex (871–99), their attacks began again after his death, and Canute (1016–35) ruled England together with Norway and Denmark. Upon Canute's death, however, his empire collapsed, and the Anglo-Saxons were able to restore their dynasty upon the English throne. Soon afterwards England was conquered by the Normans, who were originally Norsemen who had settled around the Seine valley, adopted Christianity and the French language, and established the powerful dukedom of Normandy. William, Duke of Normandy, invaded England in 1066, defeating the Anglo-Saxon king, Harold, at Hastings. Thenceforth called the Con-

PLATES, *from top to bottom:* Church at Parthenay-le-Vieux; example of Romanesque style. – Cathedral of St Sophia, Novgorod. – The Emperor Henry IV at Canossa. – Supporters of the Holy Roman Emperor fighting against the Guelphs in Rome.

17

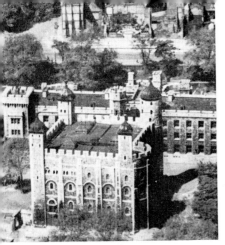

queror, he was crowned at London, where the Tower was built as a palace and fortress. The Bayeux Tapestry gives us a vivid picture of William's expedition; it was woven as a kind of justification for his action. He established a powerful centralised authority, made the valuation survey of England known as the Domesday Book, but gave his Norman-French knights such a preponderance in the government of the country that the English language and civilisation acquired a distinctly French flavour. ❧ A later dynasty, the Plantagenets, produced in the person of Henry II a monarch who acquired extensive possessions in western France (the seed from which sprang the Hundred Years War). Henry, however, came into violent conflict with the Archbishop of Canterbury, Thomas Becket, as a result of the Constitutions of Clarendon (1164), which limited the powers of the Church courts. Becket was murdered in the cathedral, and after his canonisation his tomb became the destination of many pilgrims, as we see in Chaucer's *Canterbury Tales*, written several centuries later. Moreover, Henry had to abandon some of the claims he had made in the Constitutions of Clarendon, and the problem of the relationship between Church and Crown in England remained unsettled.

France had in the Middle Ages a development which was in some respects the opposite to that of Germany. In 987 the Duke of France (i.e. of the area round Paris), Hugues Capet, ascended the throne and founded a hereditary dynasty. The fact that the kings in the first centuries had always had grown-up successors meant that the monarchy was from the start much stronger in France than in Germany. During the Middle Ages the French kings succeeded in gradually extending the royal territory, so that by about 1500 French unity was complete and the kings could initiate a policy of expansion. ❧ The evolution of France and Germany in opposite directions took place largely during the Crusades (1096–1296). When the world, contrary to popular expectation, continued to exist after the year 1000, a rejuvenation appeared to take place in Europe. The Church took the lead; Popes more powerful than those of former times restored Church discipline, supported in this task by the Cluniac Order (in Burgundy). The monastery at Cluny also led the way in the new style of building, Romanesque, which combined late reminiscences of Rome with architectural innovations from the East. Alongside the ostentatiousness of Cluny there was the sober austerity of Cîteaux. Both orders contributed much to the revival of the Church.

The Crusades. Towards the end of the tenth century the Christians had gone over to the offensive in various territories in their struggle against Islam: the *Reconquista* was in full swing in Spain, and the Saracens were also being pushed back in southern Italy and Sicily. In the East, however, the situation was less favourable. The powerful Macedonian dynasty had been followed by the Comneni as Emperors of the Byzantine Empire. They had the greatest difficulty in holding their own against the Mohammedan Seljuk tribe, who dispossessed the Eastern Romans of almost the whole of Asia Minor and placed great difficulties in the way of pilgrims in Palestine. This led to the idea of a crusade to free the Holy Land, to extend Christian efforts at expansion, so successful in the West, to the East, and perhaps to bring the Greek Orthodox Church, separated from Rome since 1054 by the Great Schism, back into the fold of Roman Catholicism. At the Council of Clermont (1095) Pope Urban II appealed to Western Christendom to seize the Holy Land from the Mohammedans. Many responded to the Pope's call under the slogan *Deus lo volt* ('God

PLATES, *from top to bottom:* The Tower of London. – Golden Codex of the Emperor Henry II (Ottonian art). – The murder of Thomas Becket. – A tournament, a favourite pastime in the Middle Ages.

18

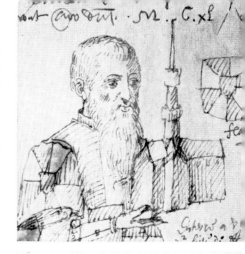

wills it'). ✤ In fact, during the First Crusade under Godfrey de Bouillon and other leaders, Jerusalem was captured in 1099 and a number of small Christian states were founded. Yet the Crusades (there was even a children's crusade in 1212) had no permanent political results. The disunion of Christians and the strength of the Mohammedan resistance, particularly under the Sultan Saladin (end of twelfth century), prevented lasting success. The rift with the Greek Orthodox Church became even greater when the Fourth Crusade (1202–4) was directed not at Jerusalem but Constantinople, which was captured and looted in a barbaric way. The victors founded a Latin Empire which survived with difficulty until 1261; then the Byzantines re-took possession of their capital. But the Eastern Roman Empire had been permanently weakened. ✤ On the other hand, the Crusades were of great cultural significance. They made the West acquainted with more advanced Mohammedan and Byzantine cultures. The coarseness which had until then been a feature of Western 'civilisation' disappeared, and a more refined knightly culture came to the fore. In architecture the ethereal Gothic style with its accent on the vertical replaced the often somewhat heavy Romanesque. ✤ On the social side the Crusades contributed to the development of trade or, in other words, of towns and the middle class. Not only the Italian but also the German and Flemish towns profited by the Crusades, which opened up new horizons.

The late Middle Ages

Political situation about 1300. When the Crusades ends, we find France with a monarchy which commands increased respect, and a fragmented Germany lacking any form of central authority (the Great Interregnum, or period without an Emperor, lasted from 1250 to 1273). In England King John was compelled by the barons in 1215 to promise in Magna Carta to respect the rights and privileges of the Church and all free men of the realm. The reign of Henry III (1216–72) saw the beginning of Parliament, when representatives of the counties and boroughs, as well as the peers, were summoned to attend upon him. ✤ Despite the Crusades the Pope had been unable to increase his power. On the contrary, Pope Boniface VIII was taken prisoner at Anagni by French knights, and his successors resided at Avignon. That is why the fourteenth century is called the time of the 'Babylonian Captivity' of the Popes (1309–77). Heresy began to raise its head in various places. In Spain, after the battle of Las Navas de Tolosa in 1212, the Moors possessed only Granada and the area round it. Yet they were able to bring even this small territory to a high pitch of development, as the Alhambra at Granada attests. Portugal, Aragon, and Castile gradually became powerful states. On the whole it can be said that the two Central European powers, the Emperor and the Pope, had been eliminated, and the national Western European states had won new strength. ✤ It becomes progressively more difficult to talk of a general medieval civilisation. About 1300 Dante wrote the *Divina Commedia* in Italian, his national language, while towards the end of the century Chaucer and Wycliffe were writing in English.

The Hundred Years War. There was also important development in France. King Philippe IV had dared to take the Pope prisoner. He also made his mark in internal politics by curtailing the power of the nobility and supporting the towns. He was the last great Capetian king; the House of Valois succeeded to the throne in 1328, and its kings pursued a policy

PLATES, *from top to bottom:* Dirk of Alsace. – Crusader castle near Palmyra. – Simon de Montfort, leader of the Crusade against the Albigenses. – Boniface VIII (fresco by Giotto).

19

which was in some respects the opposite of that of the Capetians: they favoured the nobility, often pursued an irresponsible foreign policy, and were, in a word, more 'medieval' than their predecessors. ❧ The claim of the English king, Edward III, to the French crown led to the Hundred Years War between the two countries (1337–1453). The English archers repeatedly proved more than a match for the French knights. The war also saw the introduction of a new weapon, the cannon. It was typical of the House of Valois that the French king should, in 1363, grant the vacant fief of Burgundy to his fourth son instead of attaching it to the crown as the Capetians would have done, for the powerful Burgundian vassals would naturally be enemies of their feudal lord, the French king. ❧ It was Joan of Arc who finally restored their self-confidence to the French, enabling them to continue their struggle against the English with renewed energy, even after she herself had been burnt as a witch in 1431. The war ended in 1453, the English having lost all their French possessions except Calais and the Channel Islands. ❧ France emerged from this struggle as a national state with a strengthened monarchy.

❧ For England the outcome of the war had mixed results. Since the Anglo-Norman barons had now lost their French possessions, they came to regard themselves entirely as subjects of the English Crown, and so England became more of a national state. On the other hand, the return of the armies from the Continent when the fighting was over brought times of violence and disorder to England which culminated in the Wars of the Roses. From 1485, however, the strong Tudor monarchs gave the country firm rule and re-established law and order.

Germany. The individual states in Germany were becoming steadily more important. In the north, Hanseatic leagues (federations of cities, e.g. along the Rhine and the North Sea and Baltic coasts) tried to some extent to fill the vacuum of authority. The Teutonic Knights, originally an association of German Crusaders, settled in Prussia outside Imperial territory after the Crusades and expanded their borders to the area around Reval and Riga. Bavaria, Saxony, and Brandenburg developed into virtually autonomous states. ❧ Finally, in 1273, the seven chief German rulers met to elect a new Emperor. These princes were thenceforward known as the Seven Electors. The man they chose as Emperor was a Swiss nobleman, Rudolf of Habsburg. He and his successors made it a fixed rule to concern themselves less with imperial dignity than with acquiring as much territory and power as possible for their house. Marriage was the chief means which the Habsburgs chose for the carrying out of their policy. Yet they were unable to retain power in their native country, Switzerland. In the early fourteenth century the three original Forest Cantons (Uri, Schwyz, and Unterwalden) defeated the Austrian knights. To this period belongs the legend of William Tell.

The Netherlands were coming more and more into prominence about this time. In Flanders cities flourished – Ghent, Bruges, Ypres, and many others – partly through the import of raw wool from England and the manufacture of woollen goods. The towns with their self-assured craft guilds were able to block French expansion by the battle of Courtrai in 1302. This was the first defeat ever sustained by an army of knights at the hands of an army of citizens. ❧ Prosperity on a more modest scale spread from the south to the north. In Holland Floris V favoured the towns and tried to decrease the power of the nobility. But he was murdered by a group of nobles near Muiden Castle in 1296.

PLATES, *from top to bottom:* The Cloth Hall at Ypres, rebuilt after the First World War. – Battle of Courtrai (wood carving on a chest). – Hanseatic ship of the fifteenth century. – Firearms and cannon (miniature of the Hundred Years War).

Burgundy. The Netherlands also experienced the 'autumn of the Middle Ages'. About 1400 a number of the provinces, including Flanders, were absorbed in the Duchy of Burgundy, where the court cultivated the arts (van Eyck). The Dukes of Burgundy had turned against their overlord, the French king, at the beginning of the fifteenth century, and in 1435 Philippe the Good negotiated a particularly favourable treaty. The French king, Louis IX, however, relieved of the war with the English, turned against Philippe's son and successor, Charles the Bold, who was killed at Nancy in 1477 in battle against René of Lorraine and his Swiss allies. Maximilian of Habsburg, the future Emperor, who had married Charles's daughter Marie, succeeded with much difficulty in preventing a complete dissolution of the Duchy of Burgundy. It is true that Burgundy itself reverted to the crown, but the Netherlands and Franche-Comté were retained, becoming part of the Habsburg possessions after Marie's death in 1482. ❧ The son of Maximilian and Marie, Philippe the Fair, married the daughter of Ferdinand of Aragon and Isabella of Castile, thus laying the foundation of the House of Habsburg's later power. That France, surrounded by Habsburg territories, should try to break this ring was natural. This remained the principle of French policy until about 1750.

South-west and south-east Europe. The marriage of Ferdinand of Aragon and Isabella of Castile laid the foundation of Spanish unity. This foundation was further strengthened when the last Moorish stronghold, Granada, fell in 1492. What had happened in England and France thus repeated itself here: a country's political frontiers had been made to conform with its national frontiers, and the way to foreign expansion now lay open.
❧ In Eastern Europe the days of the Byzantine Empire were numbered. Reduced to Constantinople and its immediate surroundings and entirely enclosed by Turkish territory, the Empire existed by the grace of the Sultan. The city was taken by Mohammed II in 1453. The last Roman Emperor, Constantine XI, perished in the battle, Hagia Sophia became a mosque, and shortly afterwards the city was made the capital of the Ottoman Empire under the name of Istanbul. This Empire, which had undergone great expansion since the beginning of the fourteenth century, now included a large part of Asia Minor as well as the Balkans. The Ottomans were to threaten Central Europe until far into the seventeenth century; then the decline of their Empire was to raise problems almost as great as its previous expansion.

MODERN HISTORY

The changes which took place in Europe between approximately 1450 and 1550 were so significant that historians generally take an intermediate date as the start of a new phase, Modern History, which continues until 1789, the year of the French Revolution.

Modern times

Renaissance and Humanism. In the fifteenth century the cities with their rich and powerful middle class had taken over the leadership from the nobility and clergy. The power of kings, too, had increased: relying on armies of mercenaries, assisted by artillery (a weapon that only kings could afford), they no longer needed the nobility as a fighting force. The

PLATES, *from top to bottom:* The murder of Jean the Fearless at Montereau. – The Chancellor Rolin (by Jan van Eyck). – Chalk drawing of the Emperor Maximilian (by Albrecht Dürer). – Inner courtyard of the Alhambra at Granada, built in the fourteenth century.

21

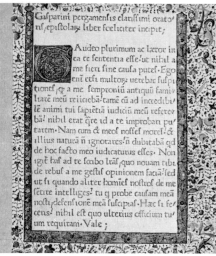

middle classes, realising the importance of a powerful central authority for trade, had supported their kings in their conflict with the nobles. This conflict, however, now turned into one between the king and the middle classes. It sometimes turned to the advantage of the king, for example in Spain and, initially, in France. In England and the Dutch Republic, however, he was eliminated, as he was finally also in France, where his power had seemed greatest. ⁊ Meanwhile, however, this new secularised non-feudal society had to find new forms of culture. In Italy scholars more or less estranged from the Church started studying the classical writers who differed so much in their outlook from medieval Christian authors. Not the supernatural but the human now came to be regarded as central to life, as it had been in antiquity. Petrarch and Boccaccio, each in his own way, had been forerunners of this view in the fourteenth century, and Byzantine scholars fleeing to Italy from the Turkish threat strengthened the movement. Kings and rich citizens, such as the Medicis of Florence, encouraged this renaissance of ancient civilisation. Nevertheless, Humanism could never have evolved into such a strong force without the invention of printing. The spirit of criticism and no doubt also the Reformation are closely associated with Gutenberg's invention. ⁊ The term Renaissance is difficult to define. Its adherents tried to make ancient art re-live; the term in fact means 'rebirth', rebirth not only of ancient civilisation but also of individualism. For the art of the ancients was not to be imitated slavishly but interpreted personally by every artist. Whereas medieval man was a member of a community (city, guild, church), the Romans and Greeks were, in the eyes of the Renaissance movement, greater individualists, and, like them, the artists of the fifteenth and sixteenth centuries wanted to live on in their work. ⁊ Brilliant names are associated with the Renaissance and Humanist period: Michelangelo, Leonardo da Vinci, and many others in Italy; Dürer and Holbein in Germany. Of the Humanists Erasmus and Thomas More must be mentioned. ⁊ Yet the period also had its less attractive sides. The undermining of Christian morals led to statesmanship of the kind advocated by Machiavelli in *The Prince*: breach of faith, assassination, and terror are perfectly permissible if only the prince attains his aim. ⁊ In general, however, the positive results of individualism and independent investigation were great. So far as science is concerned we need think only of Copernicus, who replaced the geocentric system by the heliocentric, and the great discoveries.

The voyages of discovery. Both the new spirit of inquiry and the general conditions of the age led to the discoveries. The Crusades had already shown the Genoese and Venetians the way to the East; explorers such as Willem Roebroek and Marco Polo had reconnoitred large parts of Asia. But when the Turks blocked the way to the east in the fifteenth century the maritime nations of the Mediterranean revived the idea of attacking their enemy in the rear from India. At the same time they would be eliminating an unnecessary trade link. For the Spaniards and Portuguese this merely meant a continuation of their age-old struggle against the Moors; the latter had now been driven from the Iberian peninsula, and a continuation of that struggle overseas was in line with the aims of the Crusades. Although the Portuguese undertook many voyages, such as the first circumnavigation of the world by Magellan and del Cano (1519–22), their population was not large enough to enable them to establish a large colonial empire; all they managed to found were trading stations on the coasts of Africa, Asia, and America. ⁊ The Genoese Columbus,

PLATES, *from top to bottom:* Turkish warriors (etching by Albrecht Dürer). – Page of the first book printed in Paris (1470). – Erasmus (by Albrecht Dürer). – Machiavelli, author of *The Prince*.

in the service of Ferdinand of Aragon and Isabella of Castile, based his plans on the idea that the world was round and that by sailing westwards he would arrive in India. He accidentally discovered America (1492), which, however, was named not after him but after the Italian navigator Amerigo Vespucci, who wrote about the newly-discovered continent.

❧ In their search for El Dorado, the 'Land of Gold', the Spaniards destroyed the centuries-old civilisations of the Aztecs in Mexico and the Incas in Peru. When the bishop Las Casas championed the 'Indians' who were dying in thousands in the silver mines and plantations, the only result was that the owners started importing Negro slaves from Africa. Despite the great guilt of the Spaniards in this respect, the mixture of Spanish, indigenous, and Negro blood gave rise to a new homogeneous population. A racial problem has never existed in Central and South America as it has in North America. ❧ England took little part in these discoveries, but in 1496 King Henry VII gave permission to John Cabot, a Genoese seaman, and his son Sebastian to seek a north-west passage to India. They did not succeed in doing this, but they discovered Newfoundland and its valuable fisheries for England.

The Reformation. Another result of the rise of individualism and the spirit of inquiry was the Reformation. There had been resistance to abuses in the Church towards the end of the Middle Ages, and heretical dogmas had been proclaimed, by John Hus of Bohemia, for example, who was burned to death for them during the Council of Constance (1415). Efforts to reform the Church had also been undertaken by the Brothers of the Common Life, monks who lived not in monastic isolation but in the midst of town life in order to set an example to all around them. ❧ Luther had mixed with these monks in his youth. It was not his original intention to cause a schism when in 1517 he nailed his famous 95 Theses to the doors of Wittenberg University in protest against Tetzel's trading in indulgences. He did not propose to found a new church, and when he did, he, unlike Calvin, retained as much of the old as possible. Against the Catholic Charles V, Luther relied on support from the German princes, whom he also helped in their struggle against the peasants in revolt (1525). He laid great stress on obedience to those in authority, a fact which has influenced the German national character up to our times. If the Reformation was so warmly welcomed by kings inside and outside Germany, it was partly because secularisation of monastic possessions could help to relieve the poverty of the exchequer.

Charles V. The central political figure in the first half of the sixteenth century was the Emperor Charles V, of the House of Habsburg. By his descent he was lord of a world empire: Germany, the hereditary lands in Austria, Naples and Sicily, Spain and its American possessions, the Netherlands and Franche-Comté. As a pious Catholic, he came into sharp conflict with his Protestant subjects, and as an autocratic overlord he had difficulty with the German princes. France, surrounded by Habsburg territory, obtained Turkey for an ally, so that the Emperor sometimes had to fight on three fronts. Wars at home alternated with wars abroad, and by an irony of history the Catholic Emperor was responsible for the sack of Rome in 1527, which is regarded by many as the end of the Italian Renaissance. The Turks overran the greater part of Hungary and pushed on to the gates of Vienna (1529). Despite reverses the French king François I obstinately continued his struggle against Charles, and although the final peace treaty gave the latter Flanders and Artois he

PLATES, *from top to bottom:* Statue of Marco Polo at Canton. – Columbus (by Sebastiano del Piombo). – Brazilian Indians (anonymous German woodcut, 1505). – Charles V at the Diet of Augsburg.

had not been able to recover Burgundy. Charles was equally unsuccessful in overthrowing the German Protestant princes, and the Treaty of Augsburg (1555) stated that they themselves could decide the religion of their states ('*cujus regio, illius religio*'). ꙮ A disappointed Charles abdicated in the same year. Germany's religious unity had been lost, to be followed a century later, in 1648, by its political unity. Charles's brother Ferdinand now ruled over the Austrian and German states and the narrow strip of Hungary which was still free; his son Philip II inherited Spain, the Italian and Netherlands possessions, and also the territories overseas.

The extension of the Reformation. Meanwhile the Reformation had spread to various countries during the first half of the sixteenth century, the reasons for its acceptance being often as much political as purely religious. ꙮ In England there was a growing desire for religious reform and jealousy of the wealth of the Church, but the immediate cause of the English Reformation was the Pope's refusal to grant Henry VIII a divorce from Catherine of Aragon. Papal authority was entirely abolished in England and a royal supremacy was established over the Church of England. In addition, the monasteries was dissolved and their endowments taken by the Crown. Large ruined monasteries in England still testify to wealth lost by the Church. Under Edward VI the Church of England became more Protestant and received a Prayer Book in English. Henry's daughter Mary, who was married to Philip II of Spain, attempted to restore papal power in England, but she failed; and since the reign of Henry's other daughter, Elizabeth I, the Church of England has remained an independent, established Church. ꙮ The Scandinavian countries, linked in a personal union under the Danish king since the Union of Kalmar (1397), had until now remained to some extent outside events in Europe. In the reign of Christian II, however, Sweden revolted under the leadership of Gustavus Vasa (1523), the founder of the Swedish dynasty which reigned until the beginning of the nineteenth century. Upon becoming king, Gustavus introduced Lutheranism and proceeded to confiscate Church property. He favoured the English and Dutch more than the Hanseatic League, which he feared might become too powerful, and promoted the expansion of Sweden in the Baltic area, particularly Estonia and Latvia. Denmark also adopted Lutheranism. ꙮ The latter half of the sixteenth century was to bear a somewhat different character from the first: it brought on the one hand an intensification of the Reformation by Calvinism and on the other an intensification of Catholicism by the Counter-Reformation. Violent conflicts thus became unavoidable.

Calvinism and Counter-Reformation. Luther's action opened up the way for many who wanted to put their religious individualism into practice. These smaller groups included the Zwinglians and Anabaptists; but Calvinism was of much greater significance. It flourished particularly in Geneva under the French theologian Calvin. It was radical compared with Lutheranism. Unlike Luther, Calvin taught that the relation between the Church and the state was theocratic. He expressly recognised the right of rebellion (this was put into practice in Scotland and the Netherlands). Predestination is an essential doctrine of Calvinism; Calvin moreover insisted on austerity and sobriety in his disciples. In the Netherlands, Scotland, the Palatinate, and extensive areas of southern France, Calvinism gained many converts. Colonists introduced it to New England, where it impressed its mark on society. ꙮ Meanwhile, the Catholic Church had prepared itself for a counter-offensive. The famous Council

PLATES, *from top to bottom:* Charles V's army before Ingolstadt in 1546. – Philip II, the son of Charles V, who inherited Spain and the Netherlands. – Margaret of Parma, Regent of the Netherlands. – Henry VIII of England (by Holbein).

which met at Trent between 1545 and 1563 defined doctrines, reformed abuses, and increased the Pope's power. There was no question of any concession to Protestantism: quite the contrary. While the Council stressed progress, the Jesuits contributed in large measure to the reduction of the gain of Protestantism. The Society of Jesus was founded by a former Spanish officer, Ignatius Loyola, a fervent Catholic. This Order was organised on military lines, and from this organisation and also from the learning of its members and their influential positions, for example as confessors of kings, they acquired considerable power. The set-back to Protestantism in Central Europe was largely their doing.

Political developments after 1555. A dominant figure such as Charles V had been in the first half of the sixteenth century was lacking in the second. Philip II can, it is true, be regarded as the most powerful monarch of his time, but the decline of Spain began in his reign, while Henri IV of France and Elizabeth I of England represented the rising fortunes of these countries. Much of the precious metal brought by the silver fleets flowed through Spain to the Netherlands, where Antwerp and later Amsterdam were more important centres than Cádiz and Lisbon, the latter of which belonged to Spain after 1583. Philip's successes, such as the sea battle against the Turks at Lepanto (1571), produced no results, but his failures were fatal, such as the defeat of the Armada against England (1588). ❦ England flourished greatly under Elizabeth I. Seamen, such as Frobisher, continued to search for fresh routes to India; Drake, Hawkins, and others sailed to the New World and plundered Spanish settlements there. The attempts of Gilbert and Raleigh to found colonies in North America were unsuccessful, but the establishment of the East India Company in 1600 marked the beginning of a prosperous trade with the East. Elizabeth's reign was also a great cultural period, its greatest writer being Shakespeare. Spain, as the leader of the Counter-Reformation, attempted to subdue England. The triumph of the Protestant party in Scotland led to the flight to England of Mary, Queen of Scots, who was the Roman Catholic claimant to the English throne. Elizabeth kept her in restraint until 1587, when she was executed for complicity in Roman Catholic plots. The next year brought the defeat of the Spanish Armada, which thwarted Philip II's attempt to invade England. Upon Elizabeth's death in 1603, Mary's Protestant son, James VI of Scotland, became James I of England as well, thus linking the two countries in a personal union.

France passed through a disastrous period of religious wars between 1550 and 1600. The Huguenots and Catholics were bitterly opposed to each other, the former under the leadership of families such as the Bourbons, the latter under the Guises. The dramatic climax of this struggle was St Bartholomew's Day, 1572, when countless Huguenots in Paris and elsewhere were massacred. One of the most outstanding victims was Admiral Coligny. These events caused an interruption of French aid to the rebels in the Netherlands. The civil war continued nevertheless, and Philip recalled his general Parma from the Netherlands to relieve Paris, which was being besieged by the Huguenots. Maurice of Nassau thus again obtained the opportunity to take the border fortresses in the Netherlands (1590–4). All Frenchmen finally recognised Henri de Bourbon, King of Navarre, after he had accepted Catholicism ('Paris is well worth a Mass'). The Edict of Nantes (1589) gave the Huguenots numerous privileges and for their security the *places de sûreté*. ❦ Henri IV exerted

PLATES, *from top to bottom:* Gustavus Vasa, king of Sweden. – Ignatius Loyola (ceiling painting in the Gesù, Rome). – Battle of Lepanto. – Bust of William Shakespeare at Stratford-upon-Avon.

25

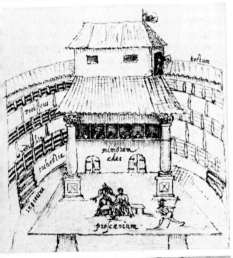

himself to the utmost to rebuild his shattered country; he may rightly be regarded as the forerunner of the great seventeenth-century French statesmen. He was assassinated in 1610 after giving his country the unity it needed for the coming French expansion.

The Netherlands passed through one of the most dramatic periods of their history in the sixteenth century. United in 1543 by Charles V, they experienced a great material and spiritual revival. It was a time of prosperity for Antwerp, where the Fuggers had their offices and Plantin had set up his printing house. ❧ Difficulties, however, began soon after Philip II's accession. A policy of centralisation met with opposition on all sides, as it had in Burgundian times: the nobility felt they had been done an injustice and the cities that their privileges had been infringed. The anti-heresy edicts were hated and feared. Emergent Calvinism acquired many followers. An economic crisis led in 1566 to an outbreak of iconoclasm, and this in turn to the arrival of Alva (1567). The Eighty Years War is considered to have begun with the unsuccessful invasion of the Netherlands by William of Orange (1568). After the fall of Antwerp in 1585 both parts of the Netherlands went their own way. The South retained an aristocratic Catholic character and the North developed into a Calvinistic democratic country where trade soon led to the emergence of a new aristocracy, the 'Regents'.

The seventeenth century

Unlike the restless sixteenth century with its unceasing political, religious, and social tensions, the seventeenth century was marked by a pronounced tendency towards authoritarianism. This development is illustrated in religion by the successes of the Counter-Reformation and in politics by the emergence of absolution. A similar trend is discerned in other fields: the rules laid down by Baroque art were obeyed as slavishly at the start of the seventeenth century as those of classicism were towards the end of the century. In economics the dominant theory was mercantilism (sometimes called Colbertism, after Louis XIV's minister, Colbert), which was intended to increase the authority of the state; that is, of the king.

The period to 1648: the Thirty Years War. In Germany the antagonism between Catholicism and Protestantism led to the Thirty Years War (1618–48), which degenerated into a struggle for power between the Emperor and the German princes, while various foreign powers intervened to turn the discomfiture of the Habsburgs to their own advantage. Sweden under King Gustavus Adolphus successfully established a foothold in northern Germany, and when France declared war on Spain and Germany in 1635 the Emperor's position became hopeless. The war came to an end in 1648 with the Peace of Westphalia. The United Netherlands and Switzerland were granted complete independence of the Empire. Sweden obtained the mouths of the great German rivers and France a large part of Alsace. The German princes, already supreme in their own principalities, were now empowered to conclude treaties with foreign powers – another step towards the disintegration of the Empire. France and Spain concluded a peace in 1659 which gave France, among other things, Artois and Roussillon.

England. James I and Charles I had continual political and religious difficulties. Parliament challenged the power of the Crown and wished

PLATES, *from top to bottom*: Admiral Coligny, leader of the Huguenots. – Woodcut portrait of Queen Elizabeth I *(British Museum)*. – Contemporary sketch of the interior of the Swan Theatre, London, 1596 *(Mansell Collection)*. – Signatures to the Union of Utrecht.

to obtain a greater share in the government of the country; the Puritans were opposed to royal control over the Church of England and wanted to make it more Protestant. This dispute led to the Civil War, which was won by the Parliamentary and Puritan forces. Charles I was executed in 1649, and the most powerful man in the country was now Oliver Cromwell, who had been largely responsible for the defeat of the Royalists. Cromwell became Lord Protector, but his attempts to establish a permanent Commonwealth brought him increasing difficulties with successive parliaments, while Puritan rule was unpopular with the people. Cromwell increased England's prestige in many ways, including his successful conduct of the First Anglo-Dutch War (1652–4), which had resulted from the protectionist Navigation Act of 1651. The Stuart monarchy was restored in 1660 with the accession of Charles II to the throne; but a lasting political settlement had yet to be reached.

France at first experienced a period of confusion after the death of Henri IV; but absolutism was firmly established by the efforts of Richelieu and Mazarin. The Estates-General were not assembled again, the Huguenots lost many of their special rights and the nobility their privileged position. Lack of a powerful middle class facilitated this process considerably, unlike the position in England where Parliament was a bulwark of civil freedom. Richelieu also interfered in German matters and by supporting the Protestants there weakened the position of the Habsburgs. Mazarin completed this work, and when Louis XIV came to the throne in 1643 he could in fact rule as an absolute monarch.

The Age of Louis XIV of France. In the second half of the seventeenth century the central figure is Louis XIV. He was absolutism personified ('*L'état, c'est moi*') and his ministers were no more than advisers. Versailles came to symbolise the glory of the *roi soleil*. ⚐ But the financial burden with which the people were saddled was disastrous and can be regarded as one of the fundamental causes of the French Revolution. He took it for granted that he was lord of all Europe, and he was fortunate in that other countries were either too weak to resist or could be bribed with subsidies. ⚐ The task of resisting France fell to the Dutch Republic. Louis tried in the course of various wars to extend his possessions, especially in the Southern Netherlands, but the Republic invariably prevented him from making great gains. On becoming stadtholder in 1672 William III successfully pursued a policy of making the Netherlands the centre of anti-French coalitions, and after his death this policy was continued by the Grand Pensionary Hensius. Louis completely exhausted his country with this succession of wars, and by the time he died in 1715 France was bankrupt. The Huguenots, distinguished for their flair for trade and industry, had been expelled by him in 1685, and this was the main factor which brought England and the Dutch Republic, both Protestant powers, together.

England's prestige abroad declined during the reign of Charles II (1660–85). The Dutch gained successes in the Second Anglo-Dutch War (1665–7), and from 1672 Charles accepted subsidies from Louis XIV in return for English neutrality during his attempt to establish French military supremacy in Europe. Charles II's political aims were to increase his own power and make Roman Catholicism stronger in the country. His reign saw the development of political parties. The Tories supported royal policy and the Whigs opposed it. Charles was succeeded by his Roman

PLATES, *from top to bottom:* Wallenstein (by Anthony Van Dyck). – Hatfield House, built in the Jacobean style. – Second seal of the Commonwealth, 1651 *(Mansell Collection)*. – Medallion head of Charles II, commemorating the Restoration, 1660 *(British Museum)*.

Catholic brother James II in 1685, the same year in which Louis XIV withdrew toleration from the Huguenots in France by the Revocation of the Edict of Nantes. Three years later a number of politicians invited William of Orange (who had married James II's elder daughter Mary) to come over from Holland with an army. James fled, and William and Mary were made by Parliament joint rulers of the kingdom. This 'Glorious Revolution' established the supremacy of Parliament and made England a constitutional monarchy. William brought England into the alliance against Louis XIV. This initiated a series of wars between England and France between 1689 and 1815. The stake at issue was mastery of the seas and the colonial possessions in America and India. England emerged victorious, thus laying the foundations of its nineteenth-century world empire. The issue was seen as early as 1715, when the Treaty of Utrecht, which ended the War of the Spanish Succession, the last war against Louis XIV, gave England Gibraltar, Newfoundland, Nova Scotia, and the Hudson's Bay territory.

The Dutch Republic. The Netherlands in this period had their Golden Age. The Dutch East India Company was importing the riches of the East; trade was enjoying a tremendous upsurge. Science and art thrived as never before and never again afterwards: the names of Rembrandt, Grotius, and Spinoza, in particular, must be mentioned. The Southern Netherlands, which remained Spanish until 1713, declined to a state of political insignificance in the seventeenth century, although it remained culturally important, as can be seen by mention of Rubens, Mercator, and Justus Lipsius. ❧ Under de Ruyter the Dutch fleet dominated the seas, as the struggle against England proved; the Four Days' Battle and the raid on Chatham (1666) are the zeniths of Dutch maritime history. Johan de Witt also intervened in the Baltic area ('The keys to The Sound are in Amsterdam'). But the prosperity of the Netherlands excited the envy of both France and England, and in 1672 the coalition of France, England, Münster, and Cologne brought the Republic to the verge of disaster. De Witt was assassinated in the same year, and while the stadt-holder William III (1672–1701) held French expansionist designs in check by his policy of maintaining European equilibrium, he also overstrained the strength of the Republic; after 1688 the Netherlands became the 'longboat behind the English frigate'. This was shown by the Treaty of Utrecht, from which they reaped scarcely any benefit.

Germany. The Empire no longer played a leading part after 1648, but the individual states came more and more to the forefront. Protestant Brandenburg-Prussia and Catholic Austria became the most important. The former became a kingdom in 1700 and was to play the role of a great power in the eighteenth century. ❧ The Austrian Habsburgs, who were continually losing ground to France in the west, were compensated for it by their conquests in the east towards the end of the century, when Turkish power declined and Hungary and Transylvania were added to their dynastic possessions, thus forming in general outline the Austro-Hungarian Monarchy, which existed until 1918.

Eastern Europe. Considerable shifts of power were taking place here. Sweden, which had become a major power in 1648, proved no match about 1700 for a Russia developing rapidly under Peter the Great, whose aim was to model his semi-Asiatic country on the West; an example of this policy was the foundation of St Petersburg (now Leningrad). It was

PLATES, *from top to bottom:* Detail of Lely's portrait of Mary II as Diana *(Mansell Collection).* – Jan Six, burgomaster of Amsterdam (by Rembrandt). – The Adoration of the Magi (by Rubens). – Louis XIV as a youth (by Le Brun).

28

under the young King Charles XII that Sweden was shattered in the struggle against the Russians. It lost all its Baltic provinces except Finland in the so-called Northern War. Russia took its place as a great power.

The eighteenth century

The growth of the modern world, cultural, economic, and political, began in the eighteenth century. The concepts of rationalism and individualism which had begun during the Renaissance developed further in England and the Dutch Republic in the seventeenth century. In the eighteenth the spirit of criticism grew stronger and the belief in human reason led to the movement known as rationalism. Closely linked to rationalism was the Industrial Revolution, which radically altered England, while with its well-developed parliamentary system it was spared the excesses of absolutism which led to the Revolution in France. ❧ In the wars of the eighteenth century Great Britain had several Continental powers as allies. ❧ Austria and Russia achieved greater and greater prominence. ❧ The Dutch Republic, though still a much desired partner because of its wealth, nevertheless experienced a relative decline in trade because the economic expansion of other countries, particularly England, proceeded much faster.

Great Britain. The Act of Union in 1707 formed the kingdoms of England and Scotland into the United Kingdom of Great Britain, which had a single Parliament as well as the same monarch. The rule of the House of Hanover began with the accession of George I in 1714. Since he did not attend cabinet meetings regularly, it became necessary to have a Prime Minister to control the cabinet and manage Parliament; and the royal ministers had generally to be appointed from the leaders of the stronger party in the House of Commons. The British constitution, with its parliamentary monarchy, political parties, and religious toleration, was a model admired by many writers in the eighteenth century, especially in France.

France. Development in France was in sharp contrast to that in Britain. Louis XV (1715–74), though not without gifts, was largely responsible for the decline of his country, not least because of his domination by a series of mistresses, of whom Madame de Pompadour is the best known but not the worst. Favouritism and waste at the court assumed unprecedented forms: 'Après moi le déluge' is a phrase attributed to Louis. ❧ Culturally, France continued to set the standard for Europe; but while this in some respects still concealed the country's weakness, in others it made it all the more obvious. ❧ The Enlightenment with its new views produced in France a number of gifted writers whose ideas were to form the breeding-ground for the Revolution. Voltaire and Montesquieu admired the example of Britain; Rousseau, from Calvinist Geneva, formulated the doctrine of the sovereignty of the people. The ideas of the Enlightenment were expressed in the *Encyclopédie* edited by Diderot and d'Alembert. ❧ A combination of enlightenment and absolutism was Enlightened Despotism, a symptom of the times, which can be summed up as: 'Everything *for*, nothing *by*, the people.'

Prussia. Germany began in the eighteenth century to recover from the disasters of the Thirty Years War. It was made culturally important by its composers and writers. Politically, however, it was individual states

PLATES, *from top to bottom:* Sir Robert Walpole, the first British Prime Minister (by Kneller) *(Mansell Collection).* – George I, from a print *(Mansell Collection).* – Anonymous bust of the stadtholder William III. – Peterhof, the residence of Peter the Great at St Petersburg.

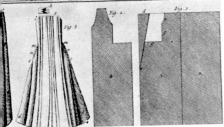

which became prominent, particularly Prussia. Frederick II of Prussia had an excellent army which he used for his policy of conquest, to which Austria fell a victim by losing Silesia (1742). This Prussian success was one of the factors which wrought a transformation in European political relations. The old opposition between France and the Habsburgs faded, because since the Peace of Utrecht the King of Spain had been a Bourbon and not a Habsburg. Fear of Prussia brought France and Austria closer together, while the hostility between France and England meant that Prussia henceforth played the role of a Continental ally of Britain (the *renversement des alliances*). Prussia, it is true, was almost shattered by the united efforts of France, Russia, and Austria in the Seven Years War (1756–63) but nevertheless managed to hold its own. In the course of this war the English drove the French from India and Canada. ❧ When Russia and Austria were convinced of Prussia's strength, the three countries got together and divided Poland among themselves in the three Partitions (1773, 1793, 1795). The Polish state disappeared, and only the fact that both Germany and Russia lost the First World War in 1918 enabled it to be restored.

The Industrial Revolution. Towards the end of the eighteenth century three revolutions took place: the Industrial, the American, and the French. The Industrial Revolution was a process which spread over several decades, and in the course of which, as the result of a number of technological inventions such as the steam engine, the spinning jenny, and the power loom, England evolved from an agricultural to an industrial state, with all attendant social consequences. The country thus obtained a lead which enabled it not only to win the wars of the eighteenth century but also to remain dominant in the nineteenth.

The American Revolution. The conquest of Canada during the Seven Years' War meant that the American colonists had less need of support from their mother country and began to assert their independence. Britain considered it necessary still to maintain troops in the colonies and wished the colonists to contribute towards the cost of their maintenance; but the colonists resented being taxed by the British government because they were not represented in Parliament. Since the British government insisted upon its right to tax the colonies and the colonists persisted in their resistance, the American War of Independence broke out. The colonists fought under the military leadership of Washington and the diplomatic leadership of Franklin until they gained their independence (1776–83). Their constitution, which was based on the principle of the sovereignty of the people, was the practical embodiment of the ideas of the Enlightenment, and for this reason it made a great impression in Europe. ❧ The British found some compensation for this loss in the consolidation of their positions in India and in the colonisation of Australia, which the voyages of Cook had made known.

France before the Revolution. When Louis XV died, he was succeeded by his grandson, Louis XVI, who was married to Marie-Antoinette, daughter of the Empress Maria Theresa. The few capable ministers who still remained, such as Turgot and Necker, were unable to avert disaster, for court intrigues soon drove them from office. Scandal followed scandal, uprisings took place for various reasons, including failure of the harvest, and it was finally decided to call the Estates-General, which had not met since 1614. It was announced that the Third Estate would have 600

PLATES, *from top to bottom:* Detail from Hogarth's portrait of his servants *(Mansell Collection).* – Diderot, one of the editors of the *Encyclopédie.* – Illustrated page on fashion from the *Encylopédie.* – Madame de Pompadour, mistress of Louis XV.

representatives, the nobility and the clergy 300 each – a recognition of the importance of the commonalty.

RECENT HISTORY

Recent history is concerned with the period from the French Revolution (1789) until the present day. The nineteenth century, partly as a result of that event and the Industrial Revolution, presents the picture of a powerful European expansion on three fronts: the social, through the emancipation of the masses; the intellectual, through the growth of science; and the geographical, through imperialism. ⟩ In the twentieth century, however, the centre of gravity moves from Western Europe. Brought to the brink of self-destruction by two wars, the continent has had to concede the leadership to non-European powers, while colonial territories have been gaining independence. ⟩ On the other hand, progressive European integration in our time has created an economic potential which ensures prosperity for all and enables Western Europe successfully to maintain its position relative to the U.S.A. and U.S.S.R.

The French Revolution and Napoleon (1789-1815)

The Revolution, which started on 5 May 1789 with the opening of the Estates-General as a struggle of the *haute bourgeoisie* against absolute royal power, originally aimed at nothing more drastic than a constitutional monarchy on the British model. For the time being the wishes of the Third Estate did not go beyond that point. But a number of dramatic events such as the storming of the Bastille (14 July 1789) and the September Massacres (1792) were indicative of an increasing shift to political radicalism, leading finally to the Terror (1793–4), a period during which many lives, including those of Louis XVI and Marie-Antoinette, were claimed by the guillotine. The fall of the Jacobin leader, Robespierre, brought this period to an end (1794). The gains of the Revolution were considerable: nationalism and liberalism emerged from it, and the equality of all men before the law, or, in other words, the end of class domination, was one of its most outstanding results. Representation of the people, compulsory education, and conscription were the means whereby the country was welded in a true national state. The abolition of local customs barriers and of local differences of law, and the new division of the country into *départements*, also gave France administrative unity. The struggle against the reactionary world around was waged with success and strengthened nationalism. A new era had begun and many even beyond France were aware of it. ⟩ When Napoleon started his career, he was the leader of the entire French nation, and this fact, together with his military genius, accounts for much of his success. And though his reign as Emperor (from 1804) may have been a reversion to an outmoded institution and more in conformity with the prevalent classicism of the time, the territories which he organised, including Belgium and the Netherlands, became modern. His campaigns spread revolutionary ideas about politics and society all over Europe. These ideas were finally to be turned against him, for example in Prussia after 1806 and in Spain after 1808. His ideal of European unity under a French hegemony was shattered by the liberal and national forces which he himself had generated. ⟩ What is more, Britain and Russia proved invincible; so far as

PLATES, *from top to bottom:* Frederick II of Prussia. – The Empress Maria Theresa, one of Frederick's chief adversaries. – Benjamin Franklin at the signing of the Declaration of Independence. – Necker, Minister of Finance under Louis XVI.

31

the former is concerned, the naval battle of Trafalgar (1805) rather than the battle of Waterloo (1815) may be regarded as the end of this second period of Anglo-French wars. The *Grande Armée* itself was annihilated in Russia (1812).

The period from 1815 to 1914

The nineteenth century can be divided into three parts. The period up to about 1848 was the time of liberation, and France in particular propagated this idea. The next period, up to 1870, was one of nationalism, especially prominent in the history of Germany and Italy. The last period, from 1870 to 1914, is characterised by imperialism, the chief exponent of which was Britain. The point of departure for the nineteenth century was the Congress of Vienna, convened to redraw the map of Europe, if possible permanently, after twenty troubled years.

The Congress of Vienna and the Restoration. It was Britain that appeared in the role of victor at the Congress of Vienna. It ruled the seas, colonies, trade, and industry, and it was further advanced politically than the rest of Europe. The Congress aimed at the restoration of traditional authorities ('legitimism'); but in the long run the modern political concepts of liberalism and nationalism proved too strong to be repressed. It was only the multi-national Austro-Hungarian monarchy which was absolutely obliged, in the interest of self-preservation, to put down all liberal and national movements; in the eyes of the Chancellor, Metternich, it was the only way of ensuring the survival of Austria. The chief provisions of the Congress of Vienna (1815) were the following: Great Britain obtained or retained Malta, Heligoland, the Cape of Good Hope, Ceylon, and part of Guiana; Austria renounced the Southern Netherlands and was given Lombardy and Venetia by way of compensation; Prussia was considerably extended but continued to consist of two separate parts; and the Holy Roman Empire was replaced by the German Confederation under Austrian leadership. The Dutch Republic made way for the Kingdom of the Netherlands (i.e. Holland and Belgium) under the House of Orange. In southern Europe old dynasties returned. Russia formed a personal union with Poland and Finland, while Sweden and Norway joined in a union of crowns. By 1820 liberalism was being pushed back on all sides. But the tide turned in the next ten years. In America, for instance, Spain was unable to recover its rebellious colonies, finding its way barred by the young, democratic United States, which, supported by Great Britain, opposed legitimist principles with the Monroe Doctrine (1823). In 1830 the Greek and Belgian nations, which had revolted, had to be given their freedom. The collapse of Metternich's system had definitely begun. The struggle for freedom was naturally promoted by the Romantic Movement. The French bourgeoisie succeeded in 1830 in expelling their reactionary king, Charles X, a brother of Louis XVI, although he had tried to distract dissatisfaction at home by occupying Algiers. He was succeeded by Louis-Philippe of Orléans, the 'bourgeois monarch'. In Britain the year 1832 saw a victory for liberalism when the Reform Bill was carried. This altered the electoral districts in such a way that the liberal industrial middle class took their place alongside the old-established country gentry in the Lower House. The Victorian age in Great Britain was to be the age *par excellence* of the middle classes, with all its advantages and disadvantages. In Russia autocracy continued throughout the reign of Nicolas I. Attempts by the Poles to regain their freedom were

PLATES, *from top to bottom:* Marie-Antoinette on her way to the scaffold. – Royalist cartoon of the Jacobin Club. – Napoleon saying farewell to his troops at Fontainebleau in 1814. – Wellington at Waterloo (detail of the picture by Pieneman).

cruelly suppressed. The country then separated itself completely from the West, and in 1848 it was the only place in Europe where quiet prevailed. Before and after 1830 Austria managed to retain its ascendency in Central Europe, not only in its own territories, but also in the German Confederation and Italy. Every expression of nationalism or liberalism was suppressed.

The period from 1848 to 1870. In 1848 Louis-Philippe was overthrown in the July Revolution by the combined forces of middle-class republicans and workers. That was the year of Marx's *Communist Manifesto*, and fear of the 'Red spectre' prevailed throughout Europe. That was why there was not much opposition in France to the dictatorship of Louis-Napoleon, the 'little nephew of a great uncle', who came to power in 1849. In 1852 he became Emperor under the title of Napoleon III. ❧ The revolutionary movement of 1848 spread to other countries, where it assumed a predominantly national character, operating centripetally in Germany, where the people wished to unite under Prussian leadership, and centrifugally in Austria, where the Czechs, Italians, and Hungarians rebelled. For a moment the Austro-Hungarian monarchy seemed about to disintegrate; the young Emperor, Franz Joseph (1848–1916), was confronted with almost insoluble problems. But the Austrians managed to assert their authority over the Czechs and Italians, and with Russian assistance the most dangerous insurgents, the Hungarians, were defeated in 1849. In fact, Austria was able, together with Russia, to call a halt to Prussian aspirations towards a united Germany (1850). ❧ But nationalism could not be stemmed. Ten years later, with support from Napoleon III and thanks to the diplomacy of Cavour, the Prime Minister of Savoy-Sardinia, Italy became a kingdom under the House of Savoy, although this did not include Venetia and Rome until 1867 and 1870 respectively. The occupation of Rome led to a conflict with the Pope, who continued until 1929 to consider himself the 'prisoner of the Vatican'. Papal authority was nevertheless considerably increased by the dogma of infallibility proclaimed in 1870. In 1866 Austria was expelled from the German Confederation, which was then dissolved to make way for a North German Confederation under Prussian presidency. This was a great success for the Prussian Chancellor Bismarck, who, however, was assisted by the fact that since 1834 the German states, excluding Austria, had been united in a customs union, the *Zollverein*. ❧ In the border regions of Europe the problems were different. Great Britain, the undisputed leading nation under Queen Victoria (1837–1901), remained aloof from European questions and concentrated on building its empire overseas. After the Indian Mutiny of 1857, the British Government abolished the East India Company, bringing India directly under the rule of the Crown and proclaiming Queen Victoria as Empress of India. Canada, on the other hand, was in 1867 the first of the colonies to obtain dominion status. The Second Reform Bill (1867) brought Britain further power along the road to complete democracy. ❧ Russia was given a feeling of strength by the assistance which it had afforded to Austria, and it determined to take possession of large parts of the Turkish Empire, including the Dardanelles. The Crimean War (1854–6), however, ended in its defeat by the combined forces of Britain, France, and Turkey. The new Tsar, Alexander II, realised that a change of policy was necessary, and in 1861 serfdom was abolished in Russia. Now that they were no longer bound to the land, many peasants migrated to the cities, where they formed the beginnings of an industrial proletariat. ❧ The American Civil War

PLATES, *from top to bottom:* Metternich, the leading personality in European politics after 1815. – James Monroe, who, together with Canning, defied Metternich. – Street fighting in Paris during the July Revolution. – Dutch troops in Brussels in 1830.

(1861–5), so often regarded as a war for the freedom of the Negro slaves, was perhaps rather a conflict between the industrial Puritan North and the agricultural, more aristocratic South. This contrast dated right from the first modest colonisations at the end of the sixteenth and beginning of the seventeenth century. The North's success, gained under the inspiring leadership of President Lincoln, meant a new era for the United States, namely emergence as a modern industrial power with its cartels and trusts. The result of the Civil War was a reverse for Napoleon III, who had hoped to create in Mexico a Catholic counterweight to the Protestant North, but was now obliged to withdraw his troops (1867). The turbulent evolution of modern states was, as we have seen, accompanied by rapidly increasing industrialism. Associated with the latter was the problem of a proletariat becoming more and more conscious of its identity: the First International was formed in 1864.

The period from 1870 to 1914. The Franco-Prussian War (1870–1), provoked by Bismarck and desired by France, put an end to French supremacy on the Continent. Napoleon III was deposed after his capitulation at Sedan, and the Third Republic was obliged to hand over the hegemony of Europe to the newly formed German Empire, which now developed into a powerful industrial state. The United States, too, was developing its industry at a rapid pace, so that Great Britain began to feel its position threatened, particularly since, unlike Great Britain, the other two countries had definitely no intention of conducting a policy of free trade. A quest for new markets and new sources of raw materials now became an essential part of British policy, and later also that of other countries. But it was Britain that developed the practice of imperialism most highly and also laid the idealistic basis for imperialism summed up in the phrase, 'the white man's burden'. ⚹ The partition of Africa began in the eighties. Britain's aim was the line from Cape to Cairo, while after the Fashoda incident (1898) France had to abandon its plans for an east-west link-up. ⚹ The Boer War (1899–1902), as an unfamiliar imperialist war against a white people, provoked violent reactions in Europe, and in consequence Britain began to feel uncomfortable in its 'splendid isolation'. ⚹ Conflicts of interests occurred in Asia after 1870 between the British and the Russians, and again in the question of the Dardanelles the British succeeded in denying the Russians access to the sea (Congress of Berlin 1878, at which the 'Big Bulgaria' proposed by Russia was reduced to a narrow strip in the Balkan peninsula). By the Congress of Berlin the British also obtained Cyprus, important because of the rights which they had recently acquired in the Suez Canal. Australia (1901), New Zealand (1907), and South Africa (1910) joined the self-governing Dominions of the British Empire. ⚹ The role played by the French in colonial matters was less spectacular: they did not wish to commit themselves too much abroad in view of a possible return match with Germany. They acquired Tunis (1881) and Morocco (1907) in North Africa, as well as the adjoining parts of the Sahara, and territories in Central Africa. Indo-China and Madagascar were also added to their possessions. ⚹ The late starters in the race for Africa, such as Germany and Italy, obtained only the deserts. ⚹ In international European politics the alliances were slowly evolved which determined the power grouping in 1914. Austria and Germany formed the Dual Alliance in 1879, while France and Russia concluded a treaty in 1893. Britain and France did not come together till 1904, nor did Britain and Russia reach an understanding until 1907, after Russia's war with the Japanese (1904–5) had revealed its weakness

PLATES, *from top to bottom:* Newsboy of 1848. – Karl Marx, the father of scientific Socialism. – Session of the Frankfurt Parliament in 1848. – Cookhouse of the 8th Hussars, a photograph from the Crimean War *(Radio Times Hulton Picture Library).*

This war, the first in which a white power suffered defeat at the hands of a non-white power, may be regarded as the beginning of Asian nationalism. That Japan, not opened up until 1854, would develop so quickly as to be able to defeat Russia had not been foreseen by any one. The continent of Asia, which had never really been colonised beyond its border regions, turned hostile to Europeans. In China, which was in a process of disintegration in the nineteenth century, there were violent outbursts of xenophobia, such as the Boxer Rising (1900), and a national revolution under Sun Yat-Sen in 1912 put an end to the fossilised régime of the Manchu Emperors. National feeling awakened in India and other colonial possessions. While Japan was busy increasing its empire (taking Korea and Formosa from China in 1895), the United States, which had seen its frontier coincide with the Pacific coast about 1900, adopted a policy of active expansion, occupying the Hawaiian Islands and the Philippines and establishing a relation of guardianship in respect of Cuba (1898). Behind the more or less local European, African, and Asiatic conflicts the world conflicts of modern times were already beginning to loom up. ❥ After 1870 the Netherlands made up their leeway. The unification of Germany, the opening of the Suez Canal, and the abolition of the colonial 'System of Cultivation' (1870) gave a great stimulus to economic life. Political and cultural activities also increased; the struggle for equality between denominational and non-denominational education ended in 1870, and the franchise was extended. The Netherlands did not participate in the race for colonies, but merely rounded off their possessions in the East Indian Archipelago.

❥ In Belgium King Leopold III personally became the sovereign of the Congo Free State (1885), which was annexed as a colony by Belgium in 1908. The first revision of the constitution in 1893 replaced the franchise by property qualification by universal plural suffrage, while the 'Equality Act' (1898) made Dutch an official language alongside French, although this did not put an end to Flemish grievances.

❥ Anti-liberal tendencies in Europe strengthened in the second half of the nineteenth century, one instance being the *Syllabus Errorum* of Pope Pius IX (1864). Advancing Socialism also constituted a threat to the liberal positions, even if only by the continuous extension of the franchise which it meant. The standard of living of the people was a matter of great importance to both Bismarck (social legislation) and Pope Leo XIII (*Encyclical Rerum Novarum*, 1891). There was no shortage of international problems in Europe: the French desire to be even with Germany, the points of Anglo-German disagreement, and the Balkans, which were in a permanent state of fermentation. But no one expected the assassination of Franz Ferdinand, successor to the Austrian throne, at Sarajevo (28 June 1914) to unleash a world war.

The First World War to the present day

The causes of the First World War were the insufficiently recognised political, economic, and psychological contrasts between the European powers, which now suddenly exploded. When the various countries had chosen sides, the Central Powers (Germany, Austria-Hungary, Bulgaria, and Turkey) formed a block stretching from the north-west to the south-east and had to fight on two fronts in Europe: the western or French front and the eastern or Russian front. In addition, the Turks fought in Iraq, Palestine, and Arabia against mainly British forces. ❥ The German attempt to eliminate France in a brief campaign by violating Belgian

PLATES, *from top to bottom:* Parade at Gettysburg in 1863, after the famous battle. – Queen Victoria of Great Britain and Ireland. – Proclamation of William I as Emperor at Versailles. – Christian de Wet, one of the generals in the Boer War.

35

neutrality failed. The war on two fronts which Germany had always feared thus became a fact. In the west hostilities developed into static warfare which, despite costly offensives (Verdun, the Somme), did not change substantially until the spring of 1918. In the east, however, the Germans made great advances against the Russians. ❧ At sea the British maintained a blockade, and the German answer to this, unrestricted submarine warfare, brought the Americans in on the Allied side in 1917. In the same year Russia collapsed as a result of the October Revolution, which brought the Communists to power under Lenin and Trotsky. They concluded the very unfavourable Treaty of Brest-Litovsk, by which Russia lost extensive regions in the west. But it was too late for the Germans. Reinforced by a steady stream of American troops, the Allies pushed the Germans back, whose own allies fell off from them, Austria-Hungary and Turkey in fact disintegrating completely. Kaiser William II had to flee to the Netherlands, and on 11 November 1918 the armistice was signed. The Peace of Versailles was to be largely based on the Fourteen Points of Wilson, the idealistic but politically inexperienced President of the United States. ❧ By the peace Germany lost all its colonies, Alsace-Lorraine, and Posen with the 'Polish Corridor' and Danzig. Austria-Hungary was divided into the separate states of Austria, Hungary, and Czechoslovakia, and lost some of its territory to Romania and a much increased Serbia, which now assumed the name of Yugoslavia. Italy acquired a certain amount of territory. Turkey retained only Asia Minor and Constantinople with the area round it.

The 'twenty years peace'. By virtue of the Fourteen Points a League of Nations was to be formed. But as the constituting act was part of the peace treaty, both victors and vanquished came to regard the League as an instrument for putting the Treaty of Versailles into effect, and since the United States reverted to isolationism and did not become a member, and Russia and Germany remained outside it, it was weak from the outset. Its imperfect organisation and the immense preponderance of the great powers prevented it from carrying out its task of promoting peace in critical moments. ❧ In Germany the Weimar Republic had great difficulties to contend with from both inflation and civil disturbances. The country was admitted to the League of Nations in 1926 and seemed set for a period of tranquillity when it was struck in 1930 by an economic crisis which had originated in America and was now making itself felt in Europe. Communism and National Socialism undermined the still weak democracy, and in 1933 Hitler seized power. He established a merciless dictatorship and immediately began to create a military machine. The situation was made worse by the fact that the great European democracies had nothing to set against it.

❧ France, which had been much weakened by the war, suffered from great political malaise after 1919 and was ruled by a succession of short-lived governments. The country believed that the construction of the Maginot Line gave it sufficient security against a repetition of 1914. ❧ In Great Britain the situation was equally unfavourable. The Labour party, which had replaced the Liberals as one of the two main parties, could not cope with the problems, and the Conservatives, who remained in power almost continuously throughout the thirties, did not do much better. Although the British Empire was now well-ordered, India under Ghandi's leadership remained in a persistent state of opposition. The very weak policy adopted towards the dictators, particularly by Chamberlain, meant a considerable loss of prestige for Britain. ❧ Italian Fascism, which had

PLATES, *from top to bottom:* Japanese warship in action during the bombardment of Port Arthur. – French troops entering Hung-Hoa (Vietnam). – The Emperor Franz Joseph of Austria-Hungary. – Pope Pius IX.

36

come to power under Mussolini in 1922, was politically active, and Mussolini's prestige was greatly increased by his treaty with Pope Pius XI (the Lateran Treaty of 1929, which made the Pope sovereign in the Vatican City); his foreign successes in 1935 confirmed his authority. Yet the rottenness of his state was revealed by the Second World War. ⁊ The Left-wing dictatorship in Russia had at first to contend with counter-revolutionary riots, famine, and foreign intervention. Lenin died in 1924, and Stalin assumed power despite Trotsky's opposition. By a harsh dictatorship Stalin tried to carry out the Five-Year Plans designed to make Russia economically strong.

The prelude to the Second World War. The situation had meanwhile deteriorated in the Far East, where Japan took advantage of China's internal difficulties under Chiang Kai-shek's régime to occupy Manchuria. Open war flared up in 1937, while relations between Japan and the United States were strained by Japanese claims to leadership in eastern Asia. Italy was emboldened to play the same game, and conquered Abyssinia in 1935, after which it joined Germany in what was called the Rome-Berlin Axis. In 1936 these two countries and Japan signed the Anti-Comintern Pact. ⁊ Hitler and Mussolini now intervened in the Spanish Civil War, which had arisen from Franco's revolt against the increasingly Leftist tendencies of the Republic. The policy of non-intervention aimed at by the Western democracies proved to be an empty gesture, and by 1939 Franco was master of the whole of Spain. ⁊ About the same time Hitler was pushing forwardly relentlessly in Central Europe, where first Austria was annexed and then, after the shameful Munich Agreement (1938), Czechoslovakia was mutilated and later annexed (1939). After Italy had occupied Albania, it was again Hitler's turn, and this time he made extortionate demands on Poland, which was already doomed to extinction by the Nazi-Soviet pact of 1939. On 1 September the Germans crossed the Polish frontier. Great Britain and France then declared war on Germany.

The Second World War. Poland was soon defeated and partitioned between Germany and Russia, which also occupied the Baltic states. In the spring of 1940 the Germans conquered first Denmark and then Norway, and a month later they overran the Low Countries, drove the British expeditionary army into the sea at Dunkirk, and, after a six weeks' campaign, forced France to capitulate. Despite aerial bombardments, however, the British held out under Churchill's leadership, but Hitler extended his power in south-east Europe by bringing Hungary, Bulgaria, and Romania into the Axis camp and conquering Greece and Yugoslavia. The Germans behaved with great cruelty: the fate of millions of Jews has laid a heavy weight on Germany's conscience. In 1941 Hitler invaded Russia; the Russians were forced to give ground for a considerable way but made a stand on the line joining Leningrad, Moscow, Stalingrad, and the Caucasus. The winter of 1943–4 saw the tide turn at Stalingrad, and from then on the Russians kept pushing back the German front. ⁊ During the same period Japan had also been winning great successes. By destroying the American fleet at Pearl Harbor (1941) the Japanese were able to occupy Burma, the Philippines, Malaya, and the Dutch East Indies almost without striking a blow. But they had underestimated the strength of the Americans under the leadership of President Roosevelt. The Battle of Guadalcanal (1942) was the turning-point of the struggle in the Pacific. ⁊ After the reconquest of Abyssinia by the

PLATES, *from top to bottom:* Belgian trench position on the Yser front. – German tanks captured by British troops. – The League of Nations Palace at Geneva. – S.A. men picketing a Jewish-owned shop.

British, the war in Africa took place mainly in the Libyan and Egyptian desert, where at the beginning of 1943 Montgomery succeeded in driving the combined German and Italian forces back. Meanwhile American troops under Eisenhower had landed in North Africa, and at the same time the Allies established air supremacy and succeeded in averting the U-boat danger. ♪ Italy capitulated after the Allied landings in Sicily and Mussolini was overthrown. The invasion of Normandy started on 6 June 1944. Three months later France, Belgium, and southern Holland were liberated. The satellite states were already beginning to defect, but Hitler struggled on, although in the east the Russians were already in Slovakia. After the Rhine was forced at several points in the spring of 1945 and the Americans and Russians had linked up on the Elbe, Hitler committed suicide during the capture of Berlin by the Russians. The surrender followed on 7 May 1945. Japan, which had been subjected to heavy aerial bombardment by the Americans, capitulated in September after two atomic bombs had been dropped. The Second World War was at an end.

The period after 1945. The period after 1945 was characterised by the continued disintegration of European authority and the consequent emancipation of African and Asian territories, as well as by an enormous increase in Soviet power, resulting in massive Russo-American rivalry, and by attempts to achieve Atlantic, or alternatively European, unity.
♪ The United Nations, established in 1944, was used by Russia as a means to achieve its aspirations in a different way. The concepts of 'Cold War' and 'peaceful coexistence' were mere slogans under which to strive for a Russian hegemony, adapted to suit the circumstances. The Russian occupation of Central and Eastern Europe led to the creation of a number of popular democracies, not all of which, however, remained under Russia's wing. Parliamentary democracy collapsed dramatically in Czechoslovakia in 1948. ♪ Stalin died in 1953. The rule of his successor Khrushchev ('destalinisation') appeared to be somewhat milder; but the way in which the Hungarian revolt was put down in 1956 proved that the régime had not changed essentially. The policy of the West had to be co-ordinated to face it. The events in Czechoslovakia led in 1949 to the formation of NATO. As the most powerful state in the West, the United States also took upon itself the economic task of helping the exhausted West, the means used being the Marshall Plan. The German occupation zones of the Allies were combined, and in 1949 the Federal German Republic was constituted under the leadership of the Chancellor Adenauer; it soon occupied an important position as an ally of the West. This, however, led to an intensification of the Cold War, as exemplified by the Berlin blockade. ♪ Much was done, and is still being done, in a variety of ways, to integrate Western Europe, the example having been set by Benelux. The ECSC (European Coal and Steel Community) was founded in 1951 and later expanded into the European Common Market.
♪ Development in Asia and Africa was everywhere accompanied by the spectacle of white rulers withdrawing, while the new states had often to contend with internal difficulties, as occurred in the Congo. Although these states were not all Communist, mistrust of the West often causes them to associate themselves with the Communist bloc, which was immensely strengthened by China's adoption of Communism, a consequence of Chiang Kai-shek's defeat by Mao Tse-tung. They also often band together to form a group of 'neutralists'. ♪ France's defeats in Indo-China and

PLATES, *from top to bottom*: Chinese students as Red Cross volunteers during the Japanese attack on China. – Spanish Government troops at Teruel during the Civil War. – Neville Chamberlain, Hitler's weak British opponent until 1940. – The Home Front in England: women working in war industry.

38

Algeria led to the fall of the Fourth Republic, which enabled de Gaulle to establish a patriarchal type of régime (1958). Great Britain granted India and Pakistan dominion status (1747) and in rapid succession emancipated large parts of its once mighty colonial empire. It withdrew from Palestine, where the new state of Israel arose, and from the Suez Canal Zone, but made a clumsy attempt in 1956 to gain a fresh footing in Egypt. In Cyprus the British reached a compromise: they retained their bases, but the island became a republic with dominion status within the Commonwealth. South Africa, however, severed connection with the Common-Wealth in consequence of its apartheid policy. Southern Ireland, Burma, and the Sudan became completely independent republics after 1945. Nevertheless, most of the liberated territories retained economic ties with Great Britain. Britain's future position in the world still remains uncertain. The new Commonwealth which has replaced the British Empire is a loosely-knit organization and does not enable Britain nowadays to rank as a great power like the United States or Russia. She can no longer act independently in foreign affairs, and in the years after the last war has, in fact, had to accept a position subordinate to America. Nor has her association with Europe yet been decided. Since 1959 she has been a member of the smaller European Free Trade Association (EFTA), but her efforts to enter the Common Market have not been successful. Somehow she must find a way of gaining a share of the large European market while retaining her Commonwealth trade and continuing to draw raw materials from overseas for her industries.

PLATES, *from top to bottom:* American soldiers capturing a Pacific island. – Allied units entering Münster. – Session of the United Nations at New York. – Russian sentries at Berlin.

Plates

These plates, with their attendant commentary, have been selected to illustrate, in general outlines, the themes more systematically covered in the maps: the ancient empires of the Near East; Greece and Rome and their heirs the Hellenistic and Byzantine civilisations; the barbarian invasions, the spread of Christianity, and the early Middle Ages, with their efforts to evolve some new political, social, economic, cultural, and spiritual values out of chaos and insecurity; the later Middle Ages, with the rise of nation states sowing the seeds of secular conflicts in Europe; the widening of physical and mental horizons and its outcome in the Renaissance and Reformation and in a new scientific and laicising attitude of mind; the political and social conflicts of the seventeenth and eighteenth centuries, with their climax in the explosion of the French Revolution and the seminal upheaval of the Napoleonic era; the nineteenth century, with its contrasts of reaction and revolution, of a middle-class utilitarian ethos with a feverish and somewhat unrealist romanticism; the world wars of the twentieth century and their aftermath of a precarious and uneasy cohabitation of conflicting ideologies. At the end are sections on Africa, America, and Asia, inevitably briefer than is ideally desirable, yet representing here also the care taken in the maps to avoid a narrowly European approach. Comparison with the list of maps will show the parallel treatment of these themes in maps and plates which enables each to illuminate the other.

EGYPT (MAP 9)

That so many records of ancient Egyptian civilisation have survived is due chiefly to the religious beliefs of the Egyptians concerning life and death. These we find reflected in the sepulchral monuments which they built for all time.

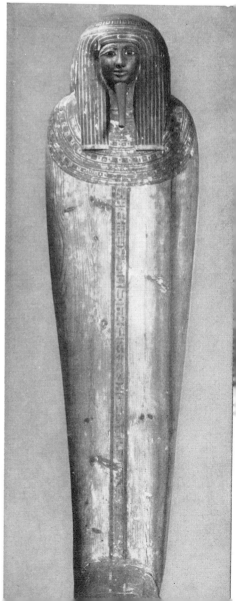

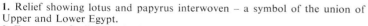

1. Relief showing lotus and papyrus interwoven – a symbol of the union of Upper and Lower Egypt.

2. Fragment of relief in a burial chamber: an outing in a rowing-boat on the Nile amidst papyrus thickets.

3. Top of an obelisk of Queen Hatshepsut (c. 1500 B.C.). She kneels before the god Amon.

4. Head of Akhenaton in relief (c. 1375 B.C.).

5. Rameses II, defeated at Kadesh in Syria by the Hittites in 1296 B.C., represented this defeat as a victory on numerous monuments. A fragment of one of these is shown here.

6. Mummy-case of Akhenaton's successor Tutankhamen (c. 1350 B.C.).

7. Part of the stele of Hammurabi (c. 1700 B.C.). The writing states that a man who steals from a burning house shall be thrown into the burning house.

The river-valley civilisation of Mesopotamia made a state and legislation necessary from a very early date, if only to ensure the maintenance of irrigation works (Pl. 7). The only building material available in the south was clay, and little has survived of the ziggurats such as the 'Tower of Babel' (Pl. 10). The Assyrians, however, had the more lasting basalt on which to perpetuate their feats of war (Pls. 8, 10).

8. Black basalt memorial column from the palace at Calah of King Shalmaneser III of Assyria (c. 840 B.C.). It illustrates his victories. The top panel shows King Jehu of Israel prostrate in the dust and offering his submission to Shalmaneser.

12. Felling the cedars of Lebanon. Detail of an Egyptian relief at Thebes. ▶

13. The sacred treasures of the Temple at Jerusalem being carried away in A.D. 70 (relief on the Arch of Titus at Rome). In the middle the *Menorah* (a seven-branched candlestick). The arch was erected to commemorate the victory of the Romans over the Jews, who had revolted.
▶

9   10

MESOPOTAMIA(MAP 9)

9. The inhabitants of the town of 'Astartu' (unidentified) being led off with their cattle by the Assyrians (relief c. eighth century B.C.).

10. Impression of a Babylonian clay cylinder-seal with representation of a ziggurat (temple tower).

11. The development of writing: Egyptian hieroglyphics, still a pictorial script; underneath, Mesopotamian cuneiform, an intermediate form; and finally, Phoenician letters.

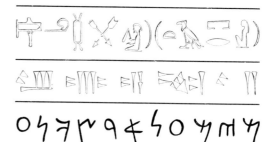

11

12   13

GREECE (MAPS 10 and 11)

While the Cretan and Mycenaean civilisations (Pls. 14, 15, 16) show a distinct relation to that of Mesopotamia, a more truly native culture developed on the mainland of Greece (Pls. 24, 25, 26) and this culture formed the basis of 'European' civilisation.

16

14

14. Cretan vases are generally decorated with animal motifs (octopus, fishes, etc.).

15. Restored part of the ruins of the palace at Cnossus in Crete. The downward-tapered Cretan columns and the stylised bull-horns are characteristic of Minoan art.

16. In the Cyclopean Wall of Mycenae in the Peloponnesus is the Lion Gate. For the column motif, cf. Pl. 15.

17. Relief showing a ship of the dead ready to cross the Styx.

18. Greek vase (c. 535 B.C.) representing Achilles and Ajax playing dice.

17

15

18

19. Archaic group from Boeotia. Women kneading dough to the accompaniment of a flute.

20. Work in progress in a bronze foundry. Left, the oven where the metal is smelted; right, the smith working on a sculpture.

21. A potter's oven filled with vases (Corinthian vase).

22. Fragment of an early geometric-pattern vase showing a war chariot.

23. The treatment of the same subject on the 'Crater of Vix' shows the advance made in technical skill and realism.

19

20

21

22   23

24. The Acropolis is dominated by the Parthenon, dedicated to the city's tutelary deity, Pallas Athena.

25. The Greeks also built temples in their colonies. A well-preserved group of buildings still stands at Paestum, south-east of Naples in what was called Magna Graecia.

26. Part of the Parthenon frieze carved by Phidias and his pupils. Three Olympian deities are shown: Poseidon, Dionysus, and Demeter.

27

28

29

HELLENISM (MAP 12)

The campaigns of Alexander the Great (Pl. 30) spread Greek civilisation to the Middle East. In the many new cities founded there arose monuments which could not fail to impress by their dimensions (Pl. 28) and their feeling for movement (Pl. 31).

27. This mosaic found at Pompeii depicts the battle of Issus at the moment when Alexander the Great attacks Darius. The latter is turning his chariot in order to flee.

28/29/30. Three antique coins showing: top, the Pharos (lighthouse) at Alexandria; centre, a statue of Nike, the goddess of victory, on the bow of a ship; bottom, an idealised portrait of Alexander.

31. The reliefs from the magnificent Altar of Zeus at Pergamum give a good idea of the Hellenistic striving after grandeur. On this fragment the goddess Pallas Athena is slaying one of the Titans, while his mother Gaea (lower right) begs in vain for mercy. Athena is being crowned by Nike, the goddess of victory.

30

31

ROME (MAP 13)

The Romans, who owed much of their civilisation to the Etruscans (Pls. 32, 33), succeeded by their talent for organisation and their military qualities in subjugating a large part of the then-known world. Under Augustus (Pl. 37) and his successors Rome became a city of magnificent palaces (Pl. 38), while new cities arose all over the Empire. From the third century onwards Roman power declined (Pl. 45); Emperors such as Diocletian and Constantine could delay this decline, but not prevent it.

32

33

32. Etruscan bronze statue of the Roman wolf. The figures of Romulus and Remus were added at a later period.

33. Etruscan cemetery at Cervetari, built over against the original city. The domed graves, which are richly decorated inside, tell us much about how the Etruscans lived.

34. Battle-elephant of King Pyrrhus of Epirus (c. 275 B.C.).

35. Hellenistic portrait of Julius Caesar.

36. Relief from Trajan's Column (c. A.D. 100). Roman soldiers with siege machines. Traces of the original paintwork survive. ▶

34

35

THE ROMAN EMPIRE

(MAP 14)

37

38

39

37. Augustus was perpetuated on numerous sculptures. He is portrayed here as Pontifex Maximus.

38. Rome. In the foreground the remains of the Circus Maximus. Behind these, the Palatine Hill with ruins of the Imperial palaces. In the background, the three arches of the Basilica of Maxentius in the Forum Romanum.

39. The Ara Pacis ('altar of peace'), built as part of Augustus' 'peace propaganda'.

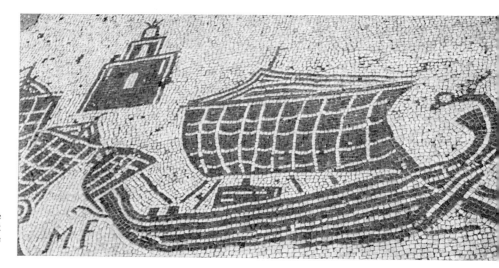

40. Mosaic from Ostia, the port of Rome: a merchant vessel passing the lighthouse (cf. Pl. 28).

41. Chariot-racing in the Forum Romanum. In the background a statue to Victoria, goddess of victory.

42. Pompeii gives an impression of a provincial town in Roman times. It was destroyed by an eruption of Vesuvius in A.D. 79.

43 44

45 46

47

43. Air photograph of Timgad (Algeria). It clearly shows how the Romans built their towns on the model of an army camp with streets intersecting at right angles.

44. The Via Appia outside Rome. The road runs in a straight line across the Campagna. Roman funerary monuments still line it.

45. When the Emperor Valerian was taken captive by the Persian king Sapor in 257 the latter had his victory perpetuated in rock reliefs in his kingdom.

46. Air photograph of Split (cf. Pl. 47). The white line outlines the palace to which Diocletian retired after his abdication.

47. Reconstruction of Diocletian's palace, now the centre of the town of Split in Yugoslavia. For the layout, cf. Pl. 43.

48. Marble head of the Emperor Constantine the Great, who granted the Christians religious liberty in 313. ▶

CHRISTIANITY

(MAP 16)

The first few difficult centuries of Christianity in Rome are known to us chiefly from the catacombs (Pl. 51). Thanks to Constantine the Great (Pl. 48) and Theodosius I it became the prodominant religion, and after the fall of the Western Roman Empire some traditions of the classics lived on in monasteries (Pl. 52).

50

51

49. The earliest known representation of Christ on the cross: a wooden door-relief at the Santa Sabina Church in Rome (early fifth century).

50. 'Name-plate' of the street of St Peter at Salona (fifth century).

51. A good idea of how early Christians lived can be obtained from the Roman catacombs, ancient Christian burial places. Shown here is the burial chamber of Marcus Claudius with its mural paintings (second century).

52. In 525 Benedict of Nursia founded his famous monastery on Monte Cassino. The strategic situation of the abbey frequently exposed it to the ravages of war, the last time being in 1944 during the Second World War. The photograph shows the restored abbey in 1956.

52

THE GERMANIC TRIBES

(MAPS 17 and 18)

Although art forms were very crude in the Early Middle Ages (Pl. 53), the memory of Rome remained alive (Pl. 54). Few of the Germanic kingdoms on former Roman soil were long-lived (Pl. 56); only that of the Franks was able to revive the Roman Imperial tradition, which it did from about 800 onwards (Pl. 55).

53

53. First page of the code of law of the Salian Franks, the 'Salic Law'. Originating under Clovis (481–511), this became famous because of the extension, by French controversialists of the fourteenth and fifteenth centuries, of its clause excluding females from the inheritance of land to their exclusion from succession to the French throne.

54. The numerous buildings which the Romans erected throughout their Empire were often put to another use after the fall of the Western Roman Empire. In Arles the amphitheatre was used as a city wall. Familiarity with Roman architecture was thus to some extent retained and influenced the form taken by the Carolingian and Romanesque styles of architecture.

55. At Rome in 800 Pope Leo III crowned Charlemagne Emperor of the Roman Empire, which was thus supposed to be restored. This mosaic in the Lateran at Rome shows the Apostle Peter handing Leo III and Charlemagne the insignia of their respective offices.

54

55

56

56. Crowns of the Visigoth kings (c. 670, found at Toledo).

BYZANTIUM (MAP 17)

In contrast to its fate in Western Europe, the Roman Empire was able to hold its own in the East. The Eastern Roman or Byzantine Empire continued to exist until 1453. It played a very important part because classical civilisation persisted there, though in Christian form, and because the Empire with its capital Constantinople for centuries remained a bulwark against the invading hordes from Asia, such as the Magyars and Turks.

58

57. Solemn transfer of the relics to the Church of Hagia Sophia built by order of Justinian in 537. Workmen are still busy on the roof. The treatment of the subject shows that the influence of ancient art was still very strong.

58. While the exterior of the Byzantine church is austere, the interior is always richly decorated with mosaics, paintings, and wrought columns. An excellent example is San Vitale at Ravenna. Between the two large pillars can be seen the famous mosaic of Justinian and his followers.

59. The Eastern Roman Empire was repeatedly afflicted with religious controversies. The most well-known of these was the controversy in the eighth and ninth centuries between those who venerated images of saints and those who desired to have no images in the churches. The illustration shows an iconoclast ('image-breaker') whitewashing a painting in a church.

60

61. The last Emperors tried again and again to obtain help from the West against Turkey. The Emperor John VIII Palaeologus journeyed to Italy in 1438, but to no avail. This mural painted in the Medici Chapel at Florence by Benozzo Gozzoli represents him as one of the Three Kings.

61

62

60. The invasions of the Balkans by Slav peoples constituted a great danger. The Slavs, however, were converted to Christianity from Constantinople and thus subjected to the cultural influence of the Eastern Roman Empire. The Emperor Michael II, 'the Stammerer' (c. 825), is here seen negotiating with the emissaries of the Bulgars.

62. Entry of the Sultan Suleiman the Magnificent (1520–66) into Constantinople at the head of his janissaries in 1526 (woodcut by Pieter Coecke of Aelst). This picture is considered one of the most reliable representations of old Constantinople. In the left background, Hagia Sophia with the hippodrome (race track) in front of it.

EUROPE THREATENED

(MAPS 16 to 20)   **(800—1050)**

After Charlemagne's death it seemed that Western Europe must be overrun. Attacks by Mohammedans (Pls. 67, 68), Slavs, Magyars (Pl. 64), Avars (Pl. 63), and Normans succeeded each other, and only in remote areas of Europe were the monasteries still able to preserve some relics of civilisation (Pl. 65).

64

65

66

63. Golden vase forming part of the 'Treasure of the Avars', found at Nagy Szent in Hungary. The decoration, consisting of motifs repeated to form strips or bands, is characteristic of the art of this people.

ISLAM

(MAP 19)

◀ **64.** In this drawing, intended as an illustration for the Book of the Maccabees, the artist has given his idea of a mounted army setting out to fight the Magyars. Only the war-elephants are foreign to the contemporary scene.

67

68

◀ **65.** An illustration from the famous Book of Kells, the work of Irish monks. The austere style of the ornamentation is typical of their art of book illumination.

◀ **66.** A good example of a Viking ship is the 'Oseberg ship', which is preserved in Oslo

67. The religious centre of the Mohammedan world is the Ka'aba at Mecca, a place of annual pilgrimage for many thousands of Muslims. The minaret of one of the mosques is visible on the left.

68. Córdoba, the capital of the Spanish Caliphate of the Ommeyads, possesses a magnificent mosque, the construction of which began in 780 and to which extensions were added in the ninth and tenth centuries. A Christian church was built in the middle of this mosque in the sixteenth century.

THE HOLY ROMAN EMPIRE (MAP 20)

69/70

In the tenth century, the Holy Roman Empire beat back the Slavs and Magyars. It also became a cultural force (Pls. 71, 75). But the Empire (Pls. 69, 70) came into conflict with the Pope (Pls. 73, 74). This and the preference of the Emperors for Italy (Pl. 76) finally led to the downfall of the Empire.

71

72

69. This crown of the Holy Roman Emperors was made in the eleventh century. It is inlaid with enamel and precious stones.

70. The Emperor Otto III (980–1002), surrounded by his spiritual and temporal advisers (contemporary miniature). His pose and clothing recall the Roman Emperors.

71. The Imperial palace at Goslar in the Harz Mountains was built in the Romanesque style. The chief characteristics of this style seen here are the low, elongated shape and the numerous rounded arches.

72. The Cluniac reform originated in the monastery of Cluny in Burgundy. The abbey, a vast building in the Romanesque style, was almost entirely demolished in 1800.

73. The remains of the castle of Canossa in northern Italy. When the Emperor Henry IV was excommunicated by Pope Gregory VII he crossed the Alps and after waiting for three days obtained admittance to the Pope, who was staying here (1077).

73

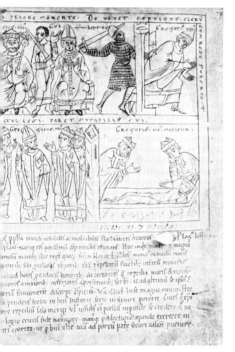

74. In this illustration from an eleventh-century chronicle the artist has depicted two episodes. In the upper half the Emperor Henry IV, with sword in hand, is putting the Pope to flight from the gates of Rome, while in the lower half we see Gregory (left) during his stay in southern Italy and (right) on his death-bed.

75. Detail of the first processional cross of the minster at Essen, showing the founders Abbess Mathilda and Duke Otto. A fine example of the art of Ottonian Germany.

74/75

76

76. Castel del Monte (Apulia) is one of the castles which the Emperor Frederick II, king of Italy and Sicily, built in the first half of the thirteenth century. It is one of the most well-preserved castles of the period.

The Crusades were another sign of Western and Central Europe's increasing power. Some of them certainly were disastrous, but the protracted stay of the Crusaders in the Holy Land (Pl. 80) caused many knights to adopt the higher and more refined culture of the Mohammedans.

77. Page from the thirteenth-century Ebulo manuscript. At the top we see Frederick Barbarossa as a participant in the Third Crusade. The middle drawing shows his death by drowning; an angel carries his soul to God. At the bottom we see the state entry of his son Henry, who succeeded in adding South Italy and Sicily to his Empire.

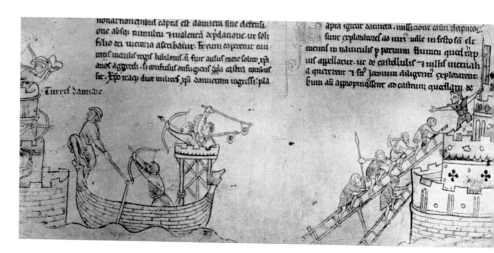

78. The siege of Damietta by a group of Crusaders in 1218–19 (from an old manuscript). The soldiers of Count William I of Holland distinguished themselves in the fighting.

79. Sculpture in Angoulême Cathedral, showing knights and archers in conflict in the period of the Crusades.

80. One of the most well-preserved Crusader castles in Syria is Krak des Chevaliers, built by the Knights of St John.

THE RISE OF THE TOWNS

(MAP 24)

The towns had been growing steadily in power since the twelfth century. It was there that the cathedrals were built (Pl. 82) and that a middle class successfully emerged.

81. As a symbol of municipal independence many cities built belfries where the charters were kept. The illustration shows the belfry (centre tower) of Ghent, completed in 1321.

82. Laon Cathedral, one of the earliest but also the most 'finished' of French Gothic cathedrals.

83. In Flanders, too, there flourished a middle-class citizen culture, and one of the forms which this took was a vigorous building industry. This late-medieval miniature gives an idea of the activity involved in building a town.

84. The city of Carcassonne. It was restored in the last century by the famous architect Viollet-le-Duc.

following page:

85. Homecoming of the remains of the French king Louis IX (St Louis), who died of the plague at Tunis in 1270. Louis's son and successor, Philippe III, follows the bier. The illustration (a fifteenth-century miniature) is also important for the details it gives of a city in the later Middle Ages.

Comment le roy Phelippe ſen retourna en france et fiſt
apporter les oz de monſƷ ſainct loys ſon pere. vliſ. chappⁱe.

Tantoſt apres que ledit roy de thunis euſt
le traittie deſſƷ eſte ſoubmis au roy charles
euſt eſte fait en onde du roy phelippe reluy
la maniere que dit eſt et q̃ roy p̃ diſpoſa ꝛ ordonna de

THE LATE MIDDLE AGES

(MAPS 25 and 28)

86. Towards the end of the Middle Ages the middle class in the towns began to take the place of the Church as the maintainer of culture. Thus Dante, a citizen of Florence, wrote his *Divine Comedy* in Italian and not in Latin, the language of the Church. The illustration shows Dante and, on the left, scenes from his work. Florence is on the right, and inside the walls it is possible to distinguish the Cathedral and the Signoria ('town hall').

87. Assisi has changed its character as a town little since St Francis walked through its streets. The photograph on the left shows the market place today, with the pillared façade of the Roman temple of Minerva, now a church, and the Palazzo del Capitano. In a fresco which he painted about 1300 in the Upper Church (right), Giotto made these buildings the background to an episode from Francis's life, in which he took the liberty of representing five instead of six columns.

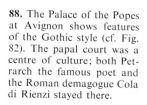

88. The Palace of the Popes at Avignon shows features of the Gothic style (cf. Fig. 82). The papal court was a centre of culture; both Petrarch the famous poet and the Roman demagogue Cola di Rienzi stayed there.

89. The Bayeux Tapestry (late eleventh century) is 231 ft. long and 20 in. wide. The section shown here represents Harold's capture after his shipwreck on the coast of France.

FRANCE AND ENGLAND (MAPS 25 and 26)

90. At the beginning of the Hundred Years War Europe was visited by a plague which brought death to nearly a third of the population. This contemporary miniature shows a mass-burial in France.

91. The Hundred Years War was in various respects a struggle between the old and the new, even with regard to methods of warfare. This English miniature shows not only the old-fashioned knight but also the modern archer and, in the background, the still more modern cannon. The fortress represents Brest during a siege by the French.

92. In 1347 Calais was taken by the English. This fifteenth-century miniature depicts the surrender of the city. On the left stands Edward III.

92

The power of France and England grew as that of the Emperor and the Pope declined. But they squandered their strength in the Hundred Years War, in which at first England was successful (Pl. 92). France was finally saved by Joan of Arc (Pls. 93, 94). The 'ancient' and the 'modern' were to be seen side by side in this war (Pl. 91).

93. Portrait of Joan of Arc drawn by a clerk during her trial. He represents her, however, as holding her sword and banner.

94

94. This tapestry represents the arrival of Joan of Arc in 1428 at the castle of Chinon, the residence of the king, Charles VII.

95. Among the cities where a powerful middle class emerged was Venice. Here arose the church of St Mark in the Byzantine style, a symbol of trade relations with the East. In the Palace of the Doge alongside it resided the Doge (the head of the municipality). The situation of the Square of St Mark on the edge of the sea illustrates the importance of commerce.

VENICE (MAPS 23, 24, and 28)

As a result of their contacts with the East (Pls. 96, 97), Genoa and particularly Venice enjoyed great prosperity, which was reflected in magnificent architecture (Pl. 95).

96. The period of the great discoveries did not in fact begin until the second half of the fifteenth century. But in the Middle Ages there was already trade between Europe and distant regions, in which the Venetians and Genoese acted as middlemen. This illustration from the *Catalan Atlas* of Charles V of France (1375) shows a caravan on its way to China.

97. Marco Polo's departure from Venice (fifteenth-century manuscript). The Polos are going by rowing-boat to their ship; in the background St Mark's and the Palace of the Doge. The objects in the foreground represent some of the countries which the Polos visited on their travels.

98 **99**

DISCOVERIES (MAP 30)

One of the great changes which mark the transition from the Middle Ages to modern times is the discovery of the ocean routes to America and Southern Asia. These events completely transformed the conception of the world, and Western Europe, from being a remote part of the world, now became its centre. The Spaniards, Portuguese, English, Dutch, and French took advantage of the opportunity, so that for centuries Western Europe was able to take the lead in world affairs.

100

98. The American Indians were powerless against the firearms of the Spaniards, as this illustration from the Codex Florentinus shows.

99. The Aztec god Quetzalcoatl, who had foretold the arrival of white men from the West.

100. By the Treaty of Tordesillas (1494) the Pope divided the world into a Spanish half and a Portuguese half. The still undiscovered Brazil became Portuguese by accident, as the line was intended to run through the Atlantic Ocean. This map of 1502, drawn for the Duke of Ferrara, is the first one to show the line.

ITALY IN THE RENAISSANCE

(MAP 28)

The Renaissance and Humanism form a second aspect of the changes which
took place in Europe about 1500. Particularly in Italy, artists drew inspiration
from antiquity (Pls. 102, 103), which they could still see around them (Pls. 101,
102). The Northern artist aimed rather at representing reality. Rome and Florence became the centre of the new movements in Italy. There was a reaction
against these movements in Florence (Pl. 107); but the Medici successfully
asserted their position there.

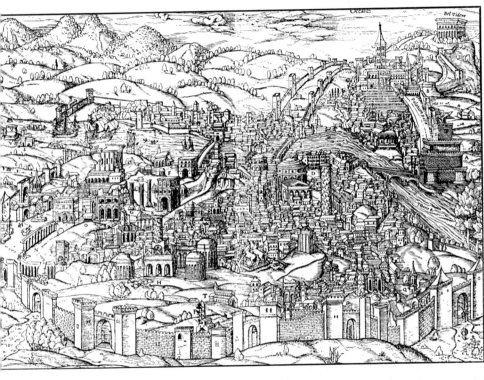

101. German woodcut of
Rome about 1500. The Pan-
theon, Trajan's Column,
Castel S. Angelo, and other
buildings of antiquity can be
clearly recognised.

102. Botticelli's Venus of
about 1500 was inspired by
a statue of Venus discovered
at this time.

103. Ghiberti's bronze reliefs for the baptistery in
Florence mark the beginning
of the Renaissance in sculpture. This one represents the
Fall of Jericho.

104. The Renaissance artist sought eagerly innovations in technique. Paolo Uccello had a preference for perspective compositions, as his 'Desecration of the Host' shows.

105. One of the finest examples of Renaissance architecture is the Church of San Biagio at Montepulciano, built by Antonio da Sangallo.

106. Pope Julius II, one of the great figures of his time portrait by Raphael).

107. The prior Savonarola denounced the licentiousness which prevailed in Florence under the Medici. He was ultimately burned outside the Palazzo Vecchio (right) in 1498.

THE REFORMATION

(MAP 32)

The Reformation and Counter-Reformation were yet other symptoms of the new era which began about 1500. Humanism, which took more practical forms in the North, was opposed to religious abuses such as the sale of indulgences (Pl. 108). The Reformation destroyed the existing unity of religion (Pls. 109, 110, 111), and the Emperor Charles V (Pl. 112) failed in his efforts to suppress Protestantism.

108. Cartoon ridiculing the friar Tetzel's trade in indulgences. The last lines run: 'The minute your coins in my coffer ring, Then straight up to heaven the souls do spring'.

109. Prominent Humanists and Reformers (painting by Lucas Cranach). In the foreground left, Luther: fourth from the right, Erasmus; extreme right, Melanchthon.

110. Portrait of Calvin in early manhood.

111. The tower of the cathedral of Münster with the cages in which the bodies of the executed Anabaptist leaders were suspended in 1538.

112. Charles V (portrait by the Venetian artist Titian). He is wearing the insignia of the Order of the Golden Fleece. ▶

EUROPE IN THE SIXTEENTH CENTURY

(MAP 31)

115

Western Europe became more and more important in the sixteenth century. Under François I (Pl. 116) France benefited by the cultural influence of Italy and produced works such as the *châteaux* on the Loire (Pl. 117); modern capitalism found an early representative in the German Jacob Fugger (Pl. 114); and England under Elizabeth I (Pl. 115) took the first step towards mastery of the seas by defeating the Armada in 1588 (Pl. 118). This was the prelude to the struggle for maritime supremacy between the powers in the seventeenth century.

113–114. The Fuggers among their other business acted as moneylenders to the House of Habsburg. They owned a very powerful branch in Antwerp. They also donated large sums to charity and in their native city of Augsburg they founded a settlement for needy townspeople, which is still called the Fuggerei.

115. Elizabeth I of England, shown in full regalia.

116. François I of France, the adversary of Charles V (drawing by Clouet).

117. François I was a patron of the arts and had a number of *châteaux* built in the Loire valley. The most well-known is that at Chambord. It still shows pronounced medieval features.

118. These prints from the British Museum show the approach of the Armada to the Channel and its engagement with the English fleet. ▶

116

117

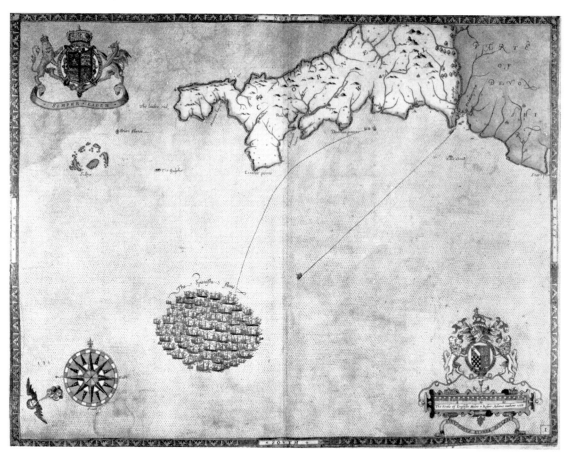

119

120

119. The Palace of Versailles, built in the reign of Louis XIV. A striking symbol of absolutism.

120. The beheading of Charles I at Whitehall, in London, in 1649.

121. William III landing at Torbay in Devonshire in 1688.

The seventeenth century was characterised by a struggle between the absolutist (Pl. 119) and the more democratic (Pls. 120, 121) forms of government, by the efforts of the West European powers to gain supremacy, and by the expansion to the east of the House of Habsburg after 1683, which to some extent compensated them for their loss of prestige after the Peace of Westphalia in 1648 (Pl. 122).

122. The Peace of West-phalia (painting by Gerard ter Borch).

123. The unsuccessful siege of Vienna by the Turks in 1683. The engraving shows that the Turks used camels as pack-animals during the siege.

124. Peter the Great (left) inspecting the building of fortifications round the projected city of St Petersburg, 'Russia's window on the West'.

125. A session of the British House of Commons about 1800. Whigs and Tories sit facing each other. William Pitt the Younger, Napoleon's great adversary, is addressing the House.

126. The 'Tobacco Club' of Frederick William I, founder of the Prussian military tradition. At the front, right, sits the future Frederick II, who while a child was obliged to attend meetings of the Club.

125

126

EUROPE IN THE EIGHTEENTH CENTURY

(MAP 38)

The chief political facts of the eighteenth century were the rise of the states – Russia and Prussia (Pls. 124, 126) – as major powers, and the struggle between England and France for mastery of the seas and the colonies, a struggle in which England was favoured by its democratic institutions (Pl. 125). But all countries experienced the effect of the Enlightenment (Pls. 127, 128, 129), which was to lead eventually to the French Revolution.

127. Sir Isaac Newton, whose investigations in mathematics and physics prepared the way for rationalism.

128. Voltaire dictating while dressing (painting by Jean Hubert).

129. The title page of the *Encyclopédie*, representing the glorification of Reason.

130. Musical life flourished in the eighteenth century. A scene from *The Marriage of Figaro* by Mozart.

127

128

129

130

THE FRENCH REVOLUTION

(MAPS 40 and 41)

The French Revolution (Pls. 131, 132) brought emancipation for the citizens but finally led to the dictatorship by Napoleon (Pl. 134), whose desire of conquest was eventually to prove his undoing (Pl. 133). Nevertheless, his campaigns spread the ideas of liberalism and nationalism over Europe.

131. Opening of the Estates-General at Versailles on 5 May 1789, with the 600 representatives of the Third Estate standing in the foreground.

132. The storming of the Tuileries on 10 August 1792. This event can be considered the fall of the monarchy.

133. The retreat of the *Grande Armée* from Russia under the leadership of Ney. This painting by Adolphe Yvon shows clearly how the later formation of the legend could confer a glow of heroism even on defeat.

134. Napoleon as Emperor (painting by David). Classical influence is very obvious here. ▶

135. The opening of
one of the first rail-
ways in England. To
judge by the back-
ground, England's
'green and pleasant
land' was already tur-
ning into the 'Black
Country'.

ENGLAND
IN THE NINETEENTH
CENTURY

In the nineteenth century Great Britain was the leading power in
the world, partly owing to its industrial lead (Pls. 135, 140). In the
Victorian age (Pl. 138), however, the distress among the working
class was very great (Pl. 137), and it was in England that Marx and
Engels formulated their revolutionary ideas (Pl. 139).

136. Robert Owen, an
industrialist, tried to
improve his workers'
social conditions by
founding a model fac-
tory; but his efforts
failed.
Top: the factory as
planned. Bottom: the
project when actually
completed.

137. The wretched
conditions of the
working classes are
clearly seen in this
drawing by Gustave
Doré, which gives a
vivid picture of life
in London slums.

138. Queen Victoria, who reigned from 1837 to 1901, became a symbol of this era. The illustration shows her inauguration at the age of eighteen.

Manifest

der

Kommuniſtiſchen Partei.

Ein Geſpenſt geht um in Europa—das Geſpenſt des Kommunismus. Alle Mächte des alten Europa haben ſich zu einer heiligen Hetzjagd gegen dies Geſpenſt verbündet, der Papſt und der Czar, Metternich nnd Guizot, franzöſiſche Radikale und deutſche Polizisten.

Wo iſt die Oppoſitionspartei, die nicht von ihren regierenden Gegnern als kommuniſtiſch verſchrieen worden wäre, wo die Oppoſitionspartei, die den fortgeſchritteneren Oppoſitionsleuten ſowohl, wie ihren reaktionären Gegnern den brandmarkenden Vorwurf des Kommunismus nicht zurückgeſchleudert hätte?

Zweierlei geht aus dieſer Thatſache hervor.

Der Kommunismus wird bereits von allen europäiſchen Mächten als eine Macht anerkannt.

Es iſt hohe Zeit daß die Kommuniſten ihre Anſchauungsweiſe, ihre Zwecke, ihre Tendenzen vor der ganzen Welt offen darlegen, und den Mährchen vom Geſpenſt des Kommunismus ein Manifeſt der Partei ſelbſt entgegenſtellen.

Zu dieſem Zweck haben ſich Kommuniſten der verſchiedenſten Nationalität in London verſammelt und das folgende Manifeſt entworfen, das in engliſcher, franzöſiſcher, deutſcher, italieniſcher, flämmiſcher und däniſcher Sprache veröffentlicht wird.

139. The condition of the working class in Britain incited Marx and Engels to publish their *Communist Manifesto* in 1848. It was published in London.

140. The Hall of Industry at the first International Exhibition in 1851. The Crystal Palace, the first large building of glass and steel, was constructed for this occasion.

NATIMALISM (MAPS 42, 43 and 45–7)

Nationalism was at first combated as a product of the French Revolution (Pl. 142) but later recognised as a factor in politics, particulary in relation to the Balkans (Pls. 141, 144). The most important new state, however, was the German Empire (Pl. 143), which took over the leadership on the Continent from France.

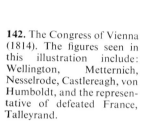

141. In this painting the French Romantic artist Delacroix expressed the despair of the Greek nation after the defeat of Missolonghi (1826).

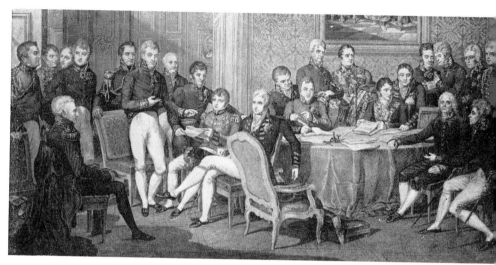

142. The Congress of Vienna (1814). The figures seen in this illustration include: Wellington, Metternich, Nesselrode, Castlereagh, von Humboldt, and the representative of defeated France, Talleyrand.

143. Capitulation of Napoleon III at Sedan in 1870. On the left, the Emperor; in the centre, William I of Prussia; and to the right of the latter, the Crown Prince and Bismarck.

144. The Congress of Berlin (1878) was held after the revolt in Bosnia and attempted both to satisfy the aspirations of the Balkan nations who were still under Turkish domination and to improve relations between Austria and Russia in the Balkans. On the left, standing, Disraeli; in the centre, the Austro-Hungarian representative Andrassy, Bismarck, and the Russian Shuvalov.

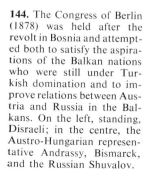

WORLD WARS

(MAPS 48–53)

The first half of the twentieth century was a period of world wars. Warfare underwent radical changes (Pls. 146, 147, 153). A second characteristic of the period was the increasing success of political extremism (Pl. 147), which attracted many followers (Pl. 148) and in which even extremes sometimes momentarily met (Pl. 150).

145–146. The First World War brought various innovations but did not affect the dominating role of infantry. Top: Belgian soldiers wearing gas-masks. Bottom: British tanks advancing on German positions.

147. A scene from the Russian Revolution in 1917: Lenin addressing soldiers and workers from a tank in St Petersburg.

150 **151**

150. The signing of the Nazi-Soviet Pact of non-aggression (23 August 1939). Standing, from left to right, Ribbentrop and Stalin; at the table, Molotov.

151. For the people of the occupied countries of Europe Churchill was the great war leader whose inspiring speeches gave millions courage, even in the most difficult times.

152

◀ **148.** National Socialism and Fascism showed a great love for mass demonstrations. In Hitler's Germany the party congress at Nürnberg was the event of the year. The photograph shows the 1938 congress, with Hitler and, on the right, Himmler, head of the S.S. and the state police.

152. The improvised quay at ▶ Dunkirk by which the defeated expeditionary British army was evacuated after the fall of France in 1940.

◀ **149.** As a result of the Munich Agreement German troops crossed the Czech border to occupy Sudetenland (3 October 1938). The frontier post still bears the Austrian colours; until March 1938 the territory had still been officially Austrian!

153

153. This photograph of the landing in June 1944 gives a clear picture of the combined use of land, sea, and air forces which was typical of the Second World War.

EUROPE AFTER WORLD WAR II

(MAPS 63 and 64)

The real winner of the Second World War proved to be the Soviet Union, which extended its power far into Central Europe. Every attempt at resistance was immediately crushed (Pl. 154). Under pressure of this threat, the West came closer and closer together; this political and economic rapprochement was reflected in associations such as NATO and EEC (Pls. 155, 156).

154. A street scene in Budapest during the rising of October 1956.

155. Germany became a member of NATO in 1959. The photograph shows Adenauer beside the French representative.

156. In 1957 the EEC and Euratom treaties were signed in Rome.

157

158

159

AFRICA

(MAP 58)

Africa, which even in antiquity had been a reservoir of slaves (Pl. 157), was not opened up by the Portuguese, who only mapped the coastal areas (Pl. 158). This task was left to various explorers in the nineteenth century (Pl. 159). The entire continent thus fell a prey to colonising European powers (Pl. 161).

157. That the original Negro inhabitants of Africa were used as slaves in very early times is shown by this Egyptian relief from the tomb of Horemheb (c. 1350 B.C.).

158. Bronze statue of a court dignitary of Benin (sixteenth century). A remarkable Negro civilisation arose in the regions of Benin and the Gold Coast, where the black population developed the art of bronze-casting. Some of their work shows European influence.

159. Discovery of Lake Tanganyika by H. M. Stanley, one of the explorers responsible for the opening up of the interior of Africa.

160. Festivities at Ismailia to mark the opening of the Suez Canal in 1869.

160

161

161. A culminating point in the Anglo-French struggle for Africa was the incident at Fashoda (1898) on the Nile. Here British troops led by Kitchener encountered a French force under Marchand. The French had to lower their flag (right).

AMERICA (MAPS 54–56)

During the decades before and after 1800 the American colonies had largely freed themselves from their British, Spanish, or Portuguese yoke (Pls. 162, 163). Attempts by the European powers to establish spheres of influence in the continent failed (Pl. 164). Of the liberated colonies, the United States developed, despite many difficult problems (Pls. 166, 167), into a leading world power (Pl. 169), which still does not enjoy the trust of its Latin-American neighbours (Pl. 168).

162. The 'Boston Tea Party' (1773). Americans disguised as Indians threw tea which had been taxed by the British Government into the harbour. This incident was the opening act of the American War of Independence (1776–83).

163. Simón Bolívar (1783–1830), the liberator of Latin America. His ideal, a unified South America, proved unattainable.

164. Attempts by France to gain a foothold in Mexico during the American Civil War failed. In 1867 the French puppet, the Emperor Maximilian of Habsburg, was executed by the Mexicans (painting by Manet).

Copy of the Engraving on the Cylinder of COLT'S U.S. Dragoons Arms.

165

166

167

168

169

165. The revolver, invented by Colt (about 1850), was a useful possession, particularly on the 'Frontier'. Its function is illustrated in this advertisement of 1865.

166. Lincoln, leader of the Northern States, at Antietam, where General Lee's advance was halted in 1862.

167. Lincoln's ideals proved difficult to realise. Even nowadays the Ku-Klux-Klan is active against Negroes, Jews, and Catholics.

168. The island of Cuba, which had been under the guardianship of America since 1898, became a centre of interest in our time through its ruler Castro openly defying the United States by, for example, his strong Soviet sympathies.

169. Immediately after the Second World War the rivalry of the United States and Russia became sharply manifest. The visit of Khrushchev to America in 1959 caused only a temporary thaw in the Cold War.

ASIA

(MAPS 33, 44, and 53)

China

170

Within the relative isolation ensured by the Great Wall of China (Pl. 170), the Chinese Empire developed a civilisation of a very high level, which had, however, become fossilised by the nineteenth century. A period of civil wars (Pl. 171) and internal unrest (Pl. 172) followed, and finally, soon after the Second World War, the Communists succeeded in seizing power.

171

170. The Great Wall of China, which for centuries kept nomadic tribes at a distance. It was completed in the reign of the Emperor Shi Hwang-ti (c. 200 B.C.).

171. Chinese print of 1911 illustrating the struggle between the Manchu forces (on left, with imperial standard) and the Republicans.

172. Europeans fleeing during the Boxer Rebellion (1900). The anti-European character of the print is obvious.

173. Speech by a woman Communist leader in Peking after the victory of the Red troops over Chiang Kai-shek. In the background, a gigantic portrait of Mao Tse-tung.

172/173

ASIA

(MAPS 44, 53, and 60)
Japan

Japan, too, had evolved its own characteristic civilisation in centuries of isolation (Pl. 176). In the nineteenth century it rapidly succeeded in mastering Western technology (Pl. 175). Unfortunately, its political aspirations led to the catastrophe of 1945 (Pl. 177).

174. Japanese passport issued to a Dutch merchant in Deshima (seventeenth century).

175. Japan, once opened up, quickly made up its technical arrears. In this woodcut made by Kyosai in 1863 we see a Japanese paddle-steamer; the sky-gods look down amazement.

176. Fourteenth-century Japanese dwelling-house. This style of building has strongly influenced modern European architecture.

177. The Japanese capitulation in 1945 to General MacArthur aboard the American battleship *Missouri* in Tokyo Bay.

ASIA

(MAP 59)

India and Indonesia

Southern and South-eastern Asia, rich in cultural traditions (Pl. 178), long remained under British and Dutch rule (Pl. 182). After 1900, however, nationalism grew in these regions (Pl. 180), and free republics sprang up after the Second World War (Pl. 183). These young states have chosen neutralism as their political ideal, but not always with success (Pl. 181).

180

178

178. Eighteenth-century painting of the Hindu god Vishnu seated on the many-headed world-serpent Ananta. At Vishnu's feet is his wife Lakshmi.

179. The Taj Mahal mausoleum, built by Shah Jehan at Agra in the seventeenth century for his wife, is a clear indication of strong Mohammedan influence in India.

180. Gandhi, the great champion of freedom for India. His policy of passive resistance was a source of considerable difficulty for the British in the period from 1918 to 1945.

181. Nehru's overtures to Communist China proved fruitless. After occupying Tibet, the Chinese invaded India in 1962. The photograph shows demonstrators at Delhi demanding the severance of diplomatic relations with Peking.

182. Visit by the Governor-General of the Netherlands East Indies, Baron Sloet van Beele, to Banjumas (c. 1865). Tropical clothing did not yet exist in those times.

183. President Sukarno addressing Indonesian youth (November 1957).

181

182

183

179

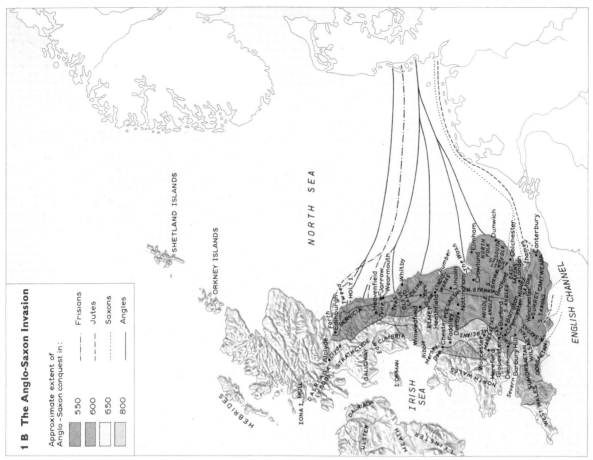

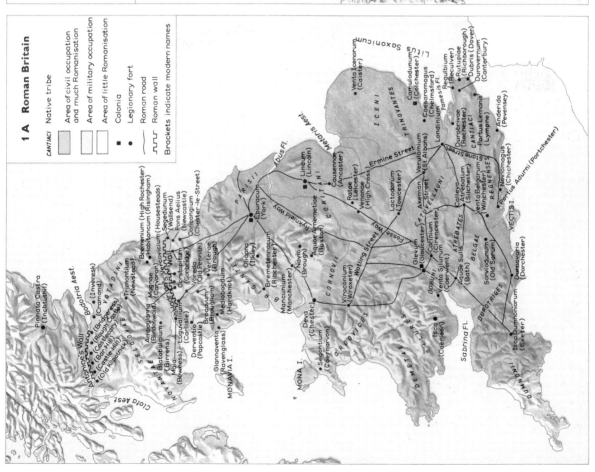

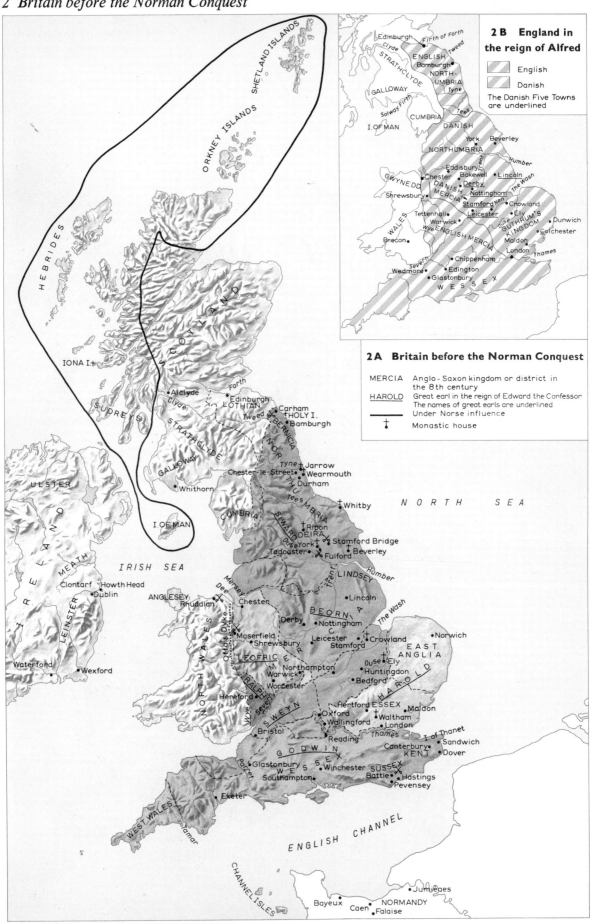

2 B England in the reign of Alfred

English
Danish
The Danish Five Towns are underlined

2 A Britain before the Norman Conquest

MERCIA — Anglo-Saxon kingdom or district in the 8th century
HAROLD — Great earl in the reign of Edward the Confessor
The names of great earls are underlined
⊦ — Under Norse influence
⊦ — Monastic house

Dover — Cinque Port
LONDON — Factory of Hansa merchants at the
Steelyard
Hull — Hansa depôt
● — Fair
✝ — Cistercian monastery
▨ — Coal
▨ — Wool
▲ — Iron
◇ — Salt

SCOTLAND

Edinburgh
Berwick
upon Tweed
Bamburgh
Alnwick
Newcastle
upon Tyne
Carlisle
Durham
Appleby
Yarm
Kendal
Scarborough
Jervaulx
Rievaulx
Fountains
Byland
York
Beverley
Hull
Grimsby
Sheffield
Flint
Chester
Boston
Derby
Grantham
Lynn
Yarmouth
Leicester
Stamford
Norwich
St Ives
Kidderminster
Stourbridge
Bury St
Edmunds
Northampton
Ipswich
Colchester
Harwich
Carmarthen
Abingdon
LONDON
Bristol
Rochester
Sandwich
Canterbury
Deal
Bridgwater
Hythe
Dover
Winchester
Rye
Romney
Taunton
Southampton
Hastings
Winchelsea
Chichester
Poole
Portsmouth
Weymouth
Dartmouth
Plymouth

4 A The British Isles in the fifteenth and sixteenth centuries

—————— Route of the Spanish Armada

·············· The English Pale in Ireland in the early 16th century

♪ Castle

O'NEILL Irish clan

<u>CLARE</u> Norman-Irish family

4 B Bishoprics before the Reformation

✝ Seat of archbishop or bishop

Diocese are named only if name is different from that of bishop's seat.

SHETLAND ISLANDS

ORKNEY ISLANDS

HEBRIDES

NORTH SEA

Caithness ✝ Dornoch

The Isles

Ross ✝ ✝ Elgin
Rosemarkie

Argyll ✝ Moray ✝ ✝ Aberdeen
Lismore ✝ Dunkeld ✝ Brechin
Iona ✝ ✝ St Andrews
✝ Dunblane
Glasgow ✝

Galloway ✝ ✝ Carlisle
Withorn ✝ Durham

Armagh ✝ Sodor and Man (to the Isles)

Tuam ✝ ✝ York
Dublin ✝
Bangor ✝ ✝ Lincoln
Cashel ✝ St Asaph ✝ Lichfield ✝
Hereford ✝ ✝ Worcester ✝ Norwich
St Davids ✝ ✝ Ely ✝ London
Bath and Wells ✝ Salisbury ✝ ✝ Rochester ✝ Canterbury
Wells ✝ Bath ✝ Winchester ✝ ✝ Chichester
Exeter ✝

SCOTLAND

• Aberdeen
Don

I. OF SKYE

MULL

Methven •
Stirling • • Perth *Tay*
Loch Menteith Dupplin Moor
Loch Leven Tantallon Castle
Falkirk • • Pinkie
ISLAY Leith ✕ Carberry Hill
Clyde Edinburgh
Glasgow • Linlithgow *Tweed* ✕ Flodden
L. OF Langside Melrose ✕ Homildon Hill
ARRAN Bothwell • Jedburgh Alnwick
Ayr • Halidon Hill
Lochmaben • Langholm ✕ • Otterburn
Solway Moss ✕ *Tyne*
Solway Firth Carlisle • Durham
Eden • Richmond
Tees
• Northallerton
TYRCONNEL
O'DONNELL *Lough Foyle* *Bann*
TYRONE Lancaster • Towton ✕ • York
O'NEILL Carrickfergus • *Ribble* Wakefield ✕ Ferrybridge • Ravenspur
BREFFNY Pontefract ✕ *Humber*
O'ROURKE I. OF MAN
O'REILLY Dundalk • *Mersey*
BURKE Kells PLUNKETT Drogheda IRISH SEA Conway ⚑ *Trent* Norwich
O'CONNOR *Boyne* Beaumaris • Rhuddlan • The Wash
Athlone Maynooth Chester Bosworth ✕ •
• Galway FITZGERALD Dublin Carnarvon • Biore Heath ✕
Kildare Kilcullen Dalkey Flint • Shrewsbury • • Fotheringhay Northampton •
O'BRIEN Rathmore W A L E S Harlech • ✕ Kenilworth *Ouse*
THOMOND O'BYRNE Tallagh Ludlow • Dudley • Warwick ✕
CLARE BUTLER Wicklow Mortimers • Worcester Colchester •
Limerick • Kilkenny OSSORY Arklow Cross • Tewkesbury ✕ St Albans ✕ Pleshey Castle
FITZGERALD *Suir* BUTLER Haverfordwest Woodstock • Barnet ✕
Blackwater CLARE • Wexford Monmouth Gloucester • Oxford •
DESMOND FITZGERALD Waterford Milford Pembroke Bristol • Windsor • London Canterbury
Lee • Cork Haven Rochester • Dover
Bandon Winchester • Hastings Rye Calais
• Kinsale Southampton • Chichester Lewes
Portsmouth •

Paris

FRANCE

ENGLISH CHANNEL

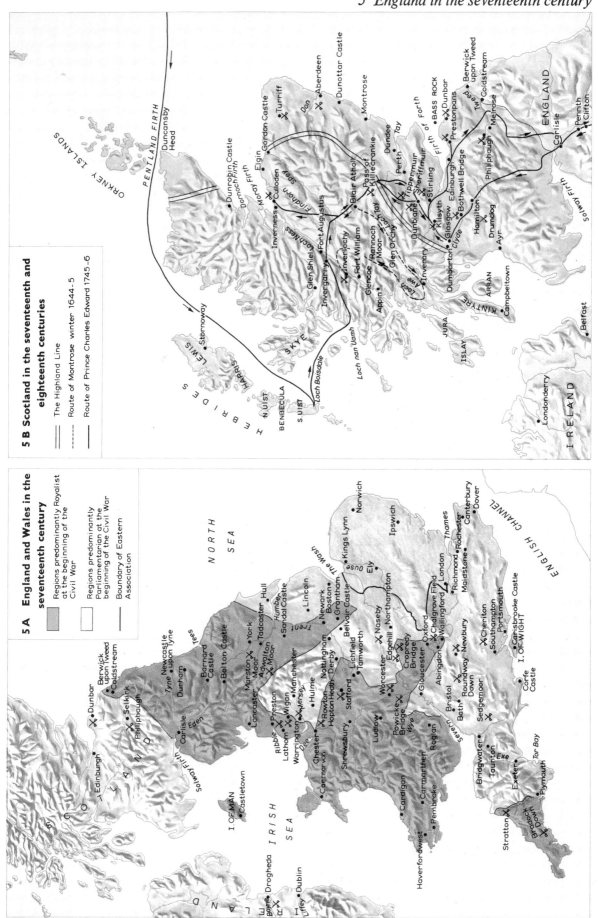

5 B Scotland in the seventeenth and eighteenth centuries

||| The Highland Line
- - - Route of Montrose winter 1644–5
——— Route of Prince Charles Edward 1745–6

5 A England and Wales in the seventeenth century

Regions predominantly Royalist at the beginning of the Civil War

Regions predominantly Parliamentarian at the beginning of the Civil War

——— Boundary of Eastern Association

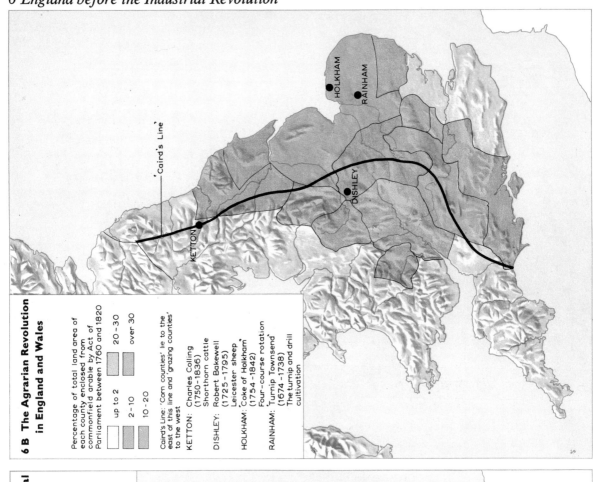

6 B The Agrarian Revolution in England and Wales

Percentage of total land area of each county enclosed from commonfield arable by Act of Parliament between 1760 and 1820

up to 2
2–10
10–20
20–30
over 30

'Caird's Line': 'Corn counties' lie to the east of this line and 'grazing counties' to the west

KETTON: Charles Colling (1750–1836) Shorthorn cattle

DISHLEY: Robert Bakewell (1725–1795) Leicester sheep

HOLKHAM: 'Coke of Holkham' (1754–1842) Four-course rotation

RAINHAM: 'Turnip Townsend' (1674–1738) The turnip and drill cultivation

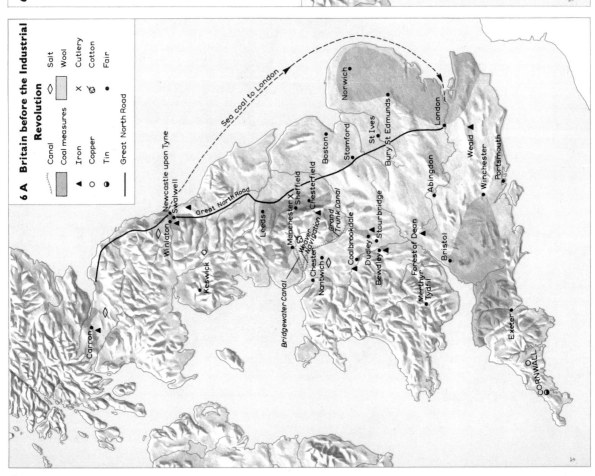

6 A Britain before the Industrial Revolution

Canal
Coal measures

Iron
Copper
Tin

Salt
Wool

Cutlery
Cotton
Fair

Great North Road

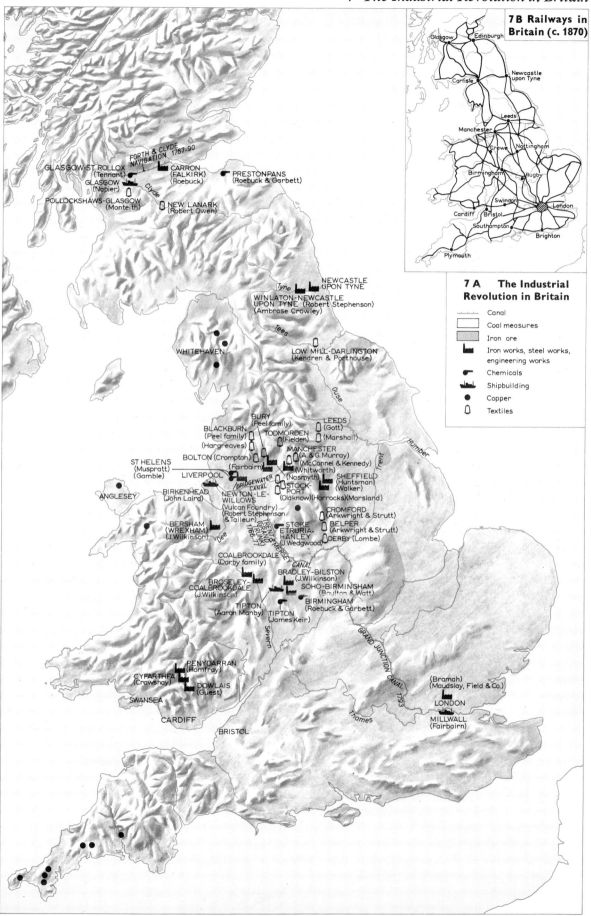

7B Railways in Britain (c. 1870)

Glasgow
Edinburgh
Newcastle upon Tyne
Carlisle
Leeds
Manchester
Crewe
Nottingham
Birmingham
Rugby
Swindon
London
Cardiff
Bristol
Southampton
Brighton
Plymouth

7 A   The Industrial Revolution in Britain

⸻⸻⸻	Canal
▭	Coal measures
▨	Iron ore
⚒	Iron works, steel works, engineering works
☙	Chemicals
⛴	Shipbuilding
●	Copper
⬚	Textiles

GLASGOW-ST ROLLOX (Tennant)
FORTH & CLYDE NAVIGATION 1767-90
CARRON (FALKIRK) (Roebuck)
GLASGOW (Napier)
Clyde
PRESTONPANS (Roebuck & Garbett)
POLLOCKSHAWS-GLASGOW (Monteith)
NEW LANARK (Robert Owen)

Tyne
NEWCASTLE UPON TYNE
WINLATON-NEWCASTLE UPON TYNE (Robert Stephenson) (Ambrose Crowley)

Tees

WHITEHAVEN

LOW MILL-DARLINGTON (Kendren & Porthouse)

Ouse

Humber

BURY (Peel family)
LEEDS (Gott)
BLACKBURN (Peel family) (Hargreaves)
TODMORDEN (Fielden)
(Marshall)
MANCHESTER (A. & G. Murray) (McConnel & Kennedy) (Whitworth)
BOLTON (Crompton)
ST HELENS (Muspratt) (Gamble)
LIVERPOOL
(Fairbairn)
(Nasmyth)
STOCK-PORT (Oldknow)
SHEFFIELD (Huntsman) (Walker)
BRIDGEWATER CANAL
(Horrocks)(Marsland)
BIRKENHEAD (John Laird)
NEWTON-LE-WILLOWS (Vulcan Foundry) (Robert Stephenson & Taileur)
ANGLESEY
CROMFORD (Arkwright & Strutt)
BELPER (Arkwright & Strutt)
BERSHAM (WREXHAM) (J.Wilkinson)
STOKE ETRURIA-HANLEY (J.Wedgwood)
DERBY (Lombe)
Dee
Mersey
Trent
COALBROOKDALE (Darby family)
BRADLEY-BILSTON (J.Wilkinson)
BROSELEY-COALBROOKDALE (J.Wilkinson)
SOHO-BIRMINGHAM (Boulton & Watt)
TIPTON (Aaron Manby)
TIPTON (James Keir)
BIRMINGHAM (Roebuck & Garbett)

Severn

GRAND JUNCTION CANAL 1793

PENYDARRAN (Homfray)
CYFARTHFA (Crawshay)
DOWLAIS (Guest)
SWANSEA
(Bramah) (Maudslay, Field & Co.)
LONDON
MILLWALL (Fairbairn)
Thames

CARDIFF

BRISTOL

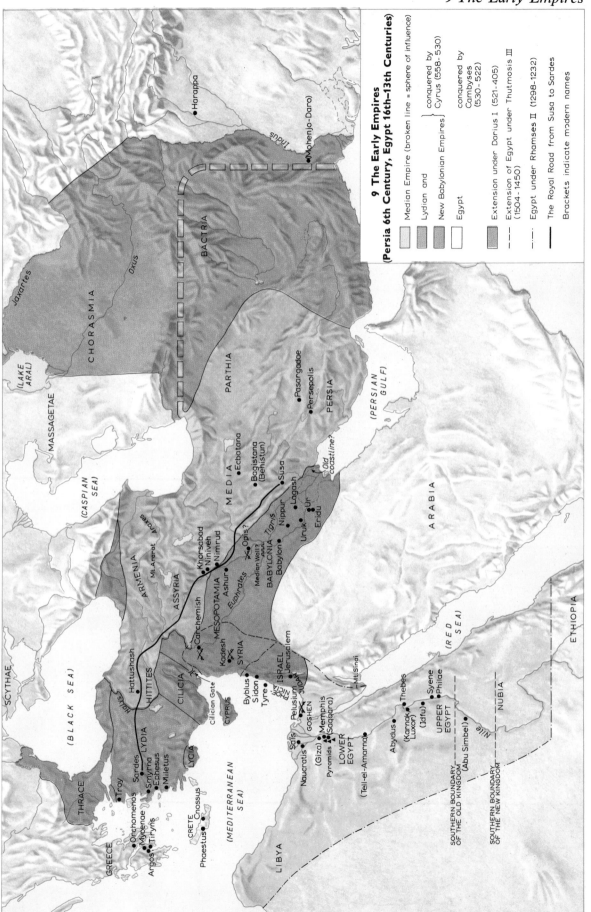

9 The Early Empires
(Persia 6th Century, Egypt 16th–13th Centuries)

Median Empire (broken line = sphere of influence)

Lydian and } conquered by
New Babylonian Empires } Cyrus (558–530)

Egypt } conquered by Cambyses (530–522)

Extension under Darius I (521–405)

—·—·— Extension of Egypt under Thutmosis III (1504–1450)

—··—··— Egypt under Rhamses II (1298–1232)

———— The Royal Road from Susa to Sardes

Brackets indicate modern names

10 Early Greece and the Persian Wars

Ionians

Aeolians

Northwest Greeks

Arcadians

Dorians

-·-·- Persian route 490

——→ Persian army 480

- -→ Persian fleet 480

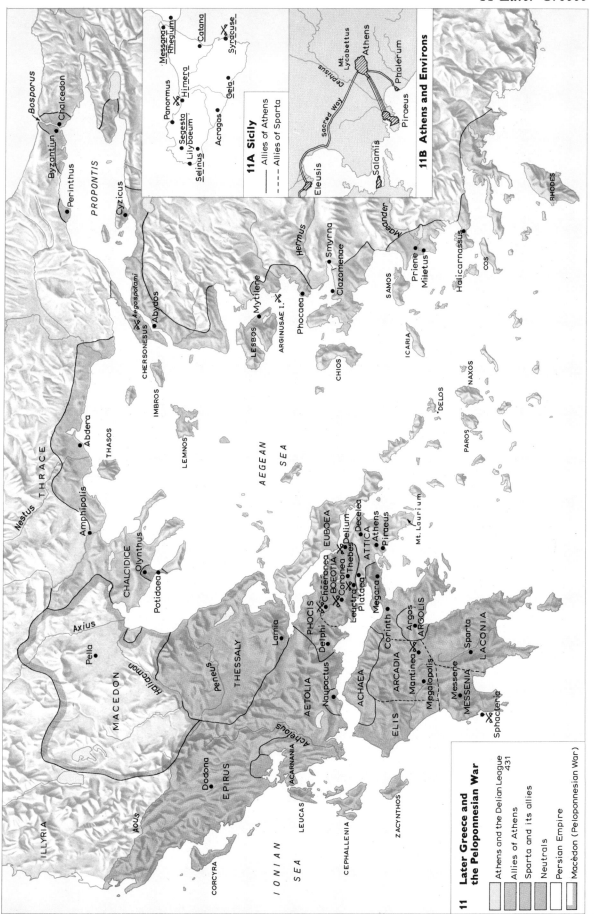

11A Sicily

Messana
Rhegium
Panormus
Himera
Catana
Syracuse
Segesta
Gela
Lilybaeum
Acragas
Selinus

— Allies of Athens
- - - Allies of Sparta

11B Athens and Environs

Cephisus
Mt. Lycabettus
Athens
Eleusis
Sacred Way
Phalerum
Piraeus
Salamis

ILLYRIA
Nestus
THRACE
Abdera
THASOS
Bosporus
Byzantium
Chalcedon
Perinthus
PROPONTIS
Cyzicus
Amphipolis
CHALCIDICE
Olynthus
Potidaea
IMBROS
CHERSONESUS
Aegospotami
Abydos
LESBOS
Mytilene
ARGINUSAE I.
Phocaea
Hermus
Smyrna
Clazomenae
SAMOS
Maeander
Priene
Miletus
Halicarnassus
COS
RHODES
LEMNOS
CHIOS
ICARIA
NAXOS
PAROS
DELOS
AEGEAN SEA

Axius
Pella
Haliacmon
MACEDON
Peneus
THESSALY
Lamia
Dodona
EPIRUS
AOUS
Achelous
ACARNANIA
AETOLIA
Naupactus
PHOCIS
Delphi
Chaeronea
Coronea
BOEOTIA
Leuctra
Thebes
Plataea
EUBOEA
Delium
Decelea
ATTICA
Athens
Piraeus
Mt. Laurium
Megara
Corinth
Argos
ARGOLIS
ACHAEA
ELIS
ARCADIA
Mantinea
Megalopolis
Messene
MESSENIA
Sphacteria
LACONIA
Sparta

IONIAN SEA
CORCYRA
LEUCAS
CEPHALLENIA
ZACYNTHOS

11 Later Greece and the Peloponnesian War

Athens and the Delian League 431
Allies of Athens
Sparta and its allies
Neutrals
Persian Empire
Macedon (Peloponnesian War)

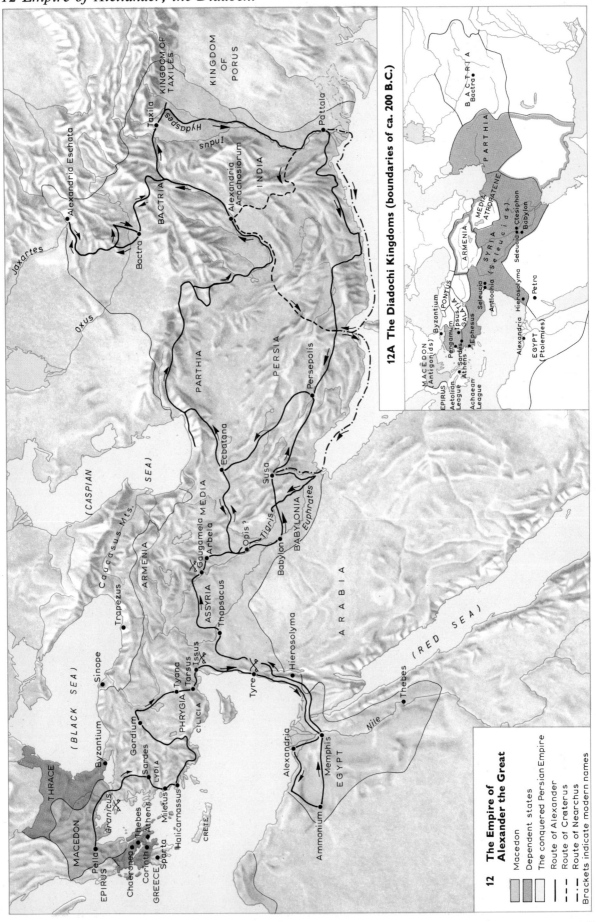

12A The Diadochi Kingdoms (boundaries of ca. 200 B.C.)

BACTRIA

PARTHIA

ARMENIA

MEDIA ATROPATENE

SYRIA (Seleucids)

Seleucia Ctesiphon

Babylon

PONTUS

Byzantium

Pergamum

PHRYGIA

GAL.

Sardes

Ephesus

Athens

Seleucia

Antiochia

Hierosolyma

Alexandria

Petra

MACEDON (Antigonids)

EPIRUS

Aetolian League

Achaean League

EGYPT Ptolemies)

Jaxartes

Alexandria Eschata

BACTRIA

Bactra

Oxus

PARTHIA

KINGDOM OF TAXILES

Taxila

Hydaspes

Indus

KINGDOM OF PORUS

Alexandria Arachosiorum

INDIA

Pattala

PERSIA

Persepolis

Ecbatana

Susa

Gaugamela MEDIA

Arbela

Opis?

Tigris

BABYLONIA

Euphrates

Babylon

(CASPIAN SEA)

Caucasus Mts.

ARMENIA

Trapezus

ASSYRIA

Thapsacus

Hierosolyma

ARABIA

(RED SEA)

Sinope

(BLACK SEA)

Byzantium

Gordium

Sardes

LYDIA

Miletus

Halicarnassus

CRETE

PHRYGIA

Tyana

Tarsus

CILICIA

Issus

Tyre

Alexandria

Memphis

EGYPT

Nile

Thebes

Ammonium

THRACE

MACEDON

Pella

EPIRUS

Granicus

Chaeronea

Thebes

Corinth

Athens

Sparta

GREECE

12   The Empire of Alexander the Great

- Macedon
- Dependent states
- The conquered Persian Empire
- - - - Route of Alexander
- –·–·– Route of Craterus
- ———— Route of Nearchus

Brackets indicate modern names

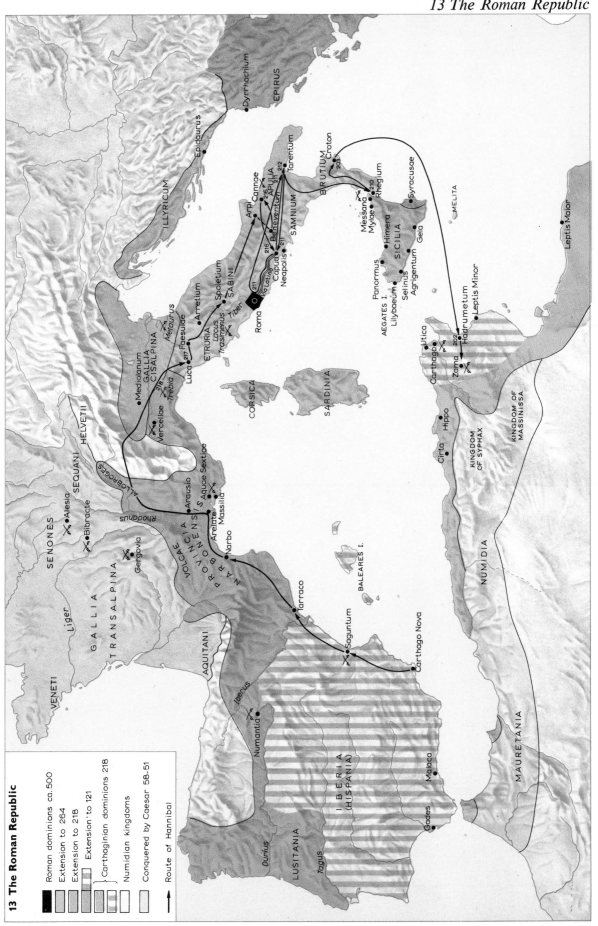

13 The Roman Republic

Roman dominions ca. 500

Extension to 264

Extension to 218

Extension to 121

Carthaginian dominions 218

Numidian kingdoms

Conquered by Caesar 58-51

Route of Hannibal

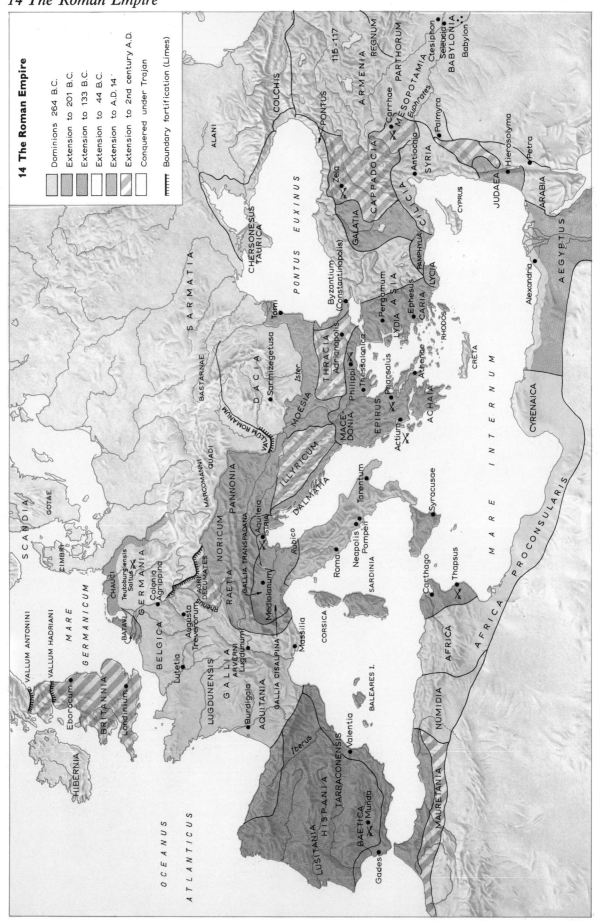

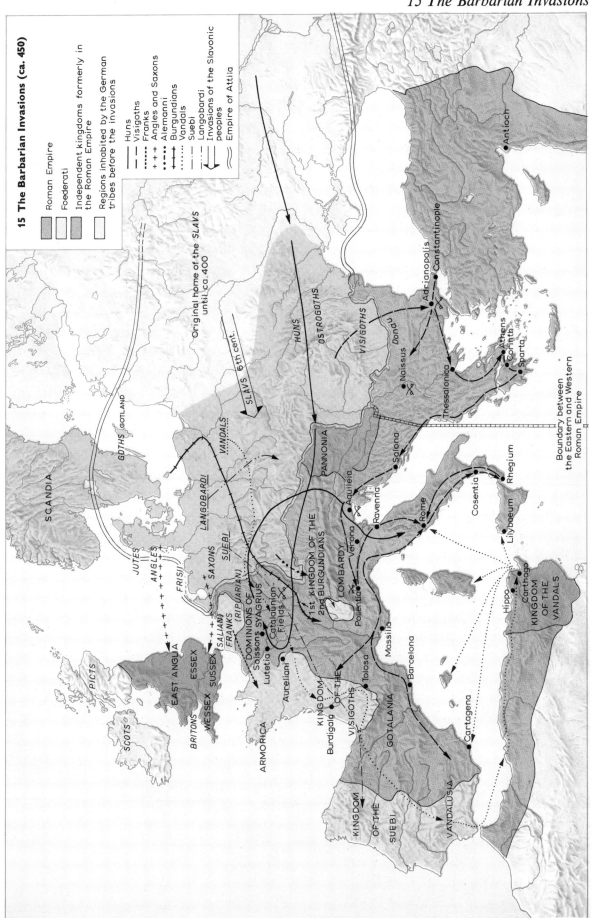

15 The Barbarian Invasions (ca. 450)

Roman Empire
Foederati
Independent kingdoms formerly in the Roman Empire
Regions inhabited by the German tribes before the invasions

Huns
Visigoths
Franks
Angles and Saxons
Alemanni
Burgundians
Vandals
Suebi
Langobardi
Invasions of the Slavonic peoples
Empire of Attila

Original home of the SLAVS until ca.400

SLAVS 6th cent.

SCANDIA

GOTHS GOTLAND

HUNS

OSTROGOTHS

VISIGOTHS

Donau

Adrianopolis
Constantinople
Athens
Corinth
Sparta
Antioch
Naissus
Thessalonica

VANDALS

LANGOBARDI

SUEBI

PANNONIA

Salona

Aquileia
Ravenna
Verona
Pollentia

LOMBARDY

Rome
Cosentia
Rhegium
Lilybaeum

JUTES
ANGLES
FRISII
SAXONS
(SALIAN) FRANKS
(RIPUARIAN)

DOMINIONS OF SOISSONS SYAGRIUS

Catalaunian Fields

1st KINGDOM OF THE
2nd BURGUNDIANS

Lutetia
Aureliani
Burdigala

PICTS
SCOTS
BRITONS
EAST ANGLIA
ESSEX
WESSEX SUSSEX

ARMORICA

KINGDOM OF THE VISIGOTHS

Tolosa
Massilia
Barcelona
Cartagena

GOTALANIA

KINGDOM OF THE SUEBI

VANDALUSIA

Hippo
Carthago

KINGDOM OF THE VANDALS

Boundary between the Eastern and Western Roman Empire

16   The Spread of Christianity

Christian in the time of Gregory I (590–604)

Converted by the death of Charlemagne (814)

Converted by the 11th century

Conquered by Islam but with a subsisting
Christian population

Conquered by Islam and wholly lost to
Christianity

Boundary between the Catholic and the
Greek Orthodox Churches after 1054

Nicaea Council
325

Rome Patriarchate

16A Palestine in the Time of Christ

Roman province of Syria

Tetrarchy of Herod Antipas
(4 B.C.–A.D. 36)

Map labels (main map):

Trondhjem, Haithabu, Lund, Gnesen, POLAND, Prague, Cracow, Gran, HUNGARY, PECHENEGS, RUSSIA (from 988), Suzdal, Novgorod, Chernigov, Kiev, Lindisfarne, York, ANGLO–SAXON KINGDOMS, Canterbury, Utrecht, Münster, Paderborn, SAXONY, Cologne, Aachen, Fulda, Trier, Mainz, Würzburg, Strasbourg, Reims, Salzburg, Paris, St. Gallen, St. Maurice, Milan, Pavia, Aquileia, Venice, CROATIA, Tirnovo, SERBIA, Okhrida, Spalato, Monte Cassino, Ravenna, Rome, Naples, Palermo, CORSICA, SARDINIA, Hippo Regius, Carthage, Tours, Poitiers, Lyon, Vienne, Arles, Toulouse, SPANISH MARCH, ASTURIAS, Santiago de Compostela, Oviedo, León, Toledo, Córdoba, Jebel Tariq, Trebizond, Theodosiopolis, ARMENIAN CHURCH, NESTORIAN CHURCH, Constantinople 381, Chalcedon 451, Nicaea 325, Iconium, Tarsus, Aleppo, Damascus, Jerusalem, Mt. Athos, Phocaea, Ephesus 431, Philippi, Thessalonica, Athens, Corinth, Antioch, Cairo, Mt. Sinai, Alexandria

Map labels (Palestine inset):

SYRIA, Damascus, Lebanon Mts., Mt. Hermon, BASHAN, PHOENICIA, Tyre, Sidon, Acco, GALILEE, Capernaum, Lake of Genesaret, Tiberias, Cana, Mt. Tabor, Nazareth, Ashtaroth, DECAPOLIS, Gilead, Gerasa, Gerasa, JEZREEL, Samaria, Shechem, Salem, Arimathea, Bethel, PERAEA, Mt. Nebo, Mt. of Olives, Jordan, Jericho, Bethany, Emmaus, Jerusalem, Bethlehem, Hebron, JUDAEA, Dead Sea, MOAB, Caesarea, Joppa, Domain of Livia and Tiberius, Ashkelon, Gaza, Beer-Sheba, Rehoboth

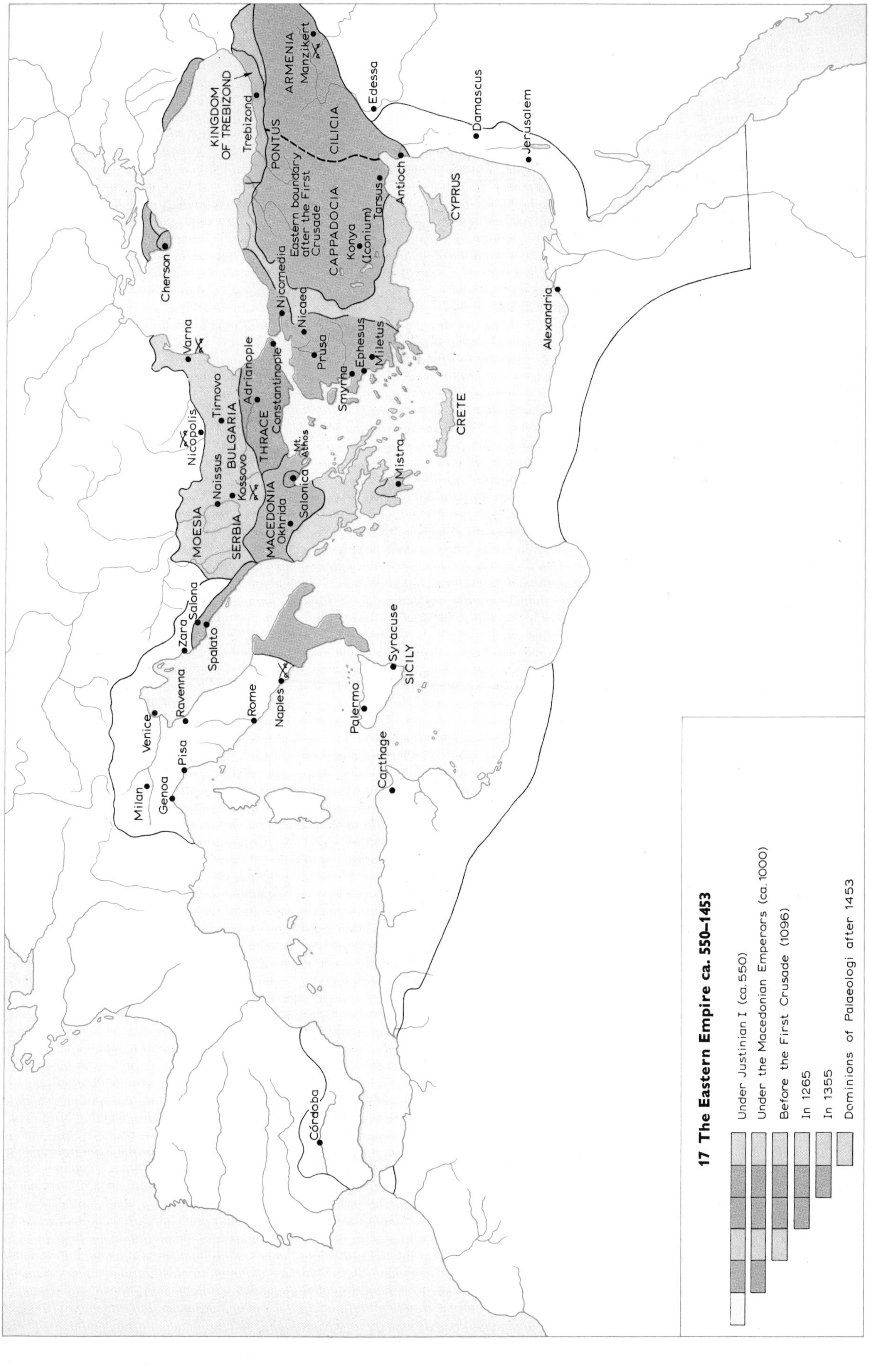

17 The Eastern Empire ca. 550–1453

Under Justinian I (ca. 550)

Under the Macedonian Emperors (ca. 1000)

Before the First Crusade (1096)

In 1265

In 1355

Dominions of Palaeologi after 1453

ARMENIA
Manzikert
Edessa
Damascus
Jerusalem
KINGDOM OF TREBIZOND
Trebizond
PONTUS
CILICIA
Eastern boundary after the First Crusade
CAPPADOCIA
Konya (Iconium)
Tarsus
Antioch
CYPRUS
Cherson
Nicomedia
Nicaea
Prusa
Ephesus
Smyrna
Miletus
Alexandria
Varna
Adrianople
Constantinople
THRACE
Tirnovo
BULGARIA
Nicopolis
Naissus
Kossovo
SERBIA
MOESIA
MACEDONIA
Okhrida
Salonica
Mt. Athos
Mistra
CRETE
Salona
Zara
Spalato
Ravenna
Rome
Naples
SICILY
Syracuse
Palermo
Carthage
Venice
Milan
Pisa
Genoa
Córdoba

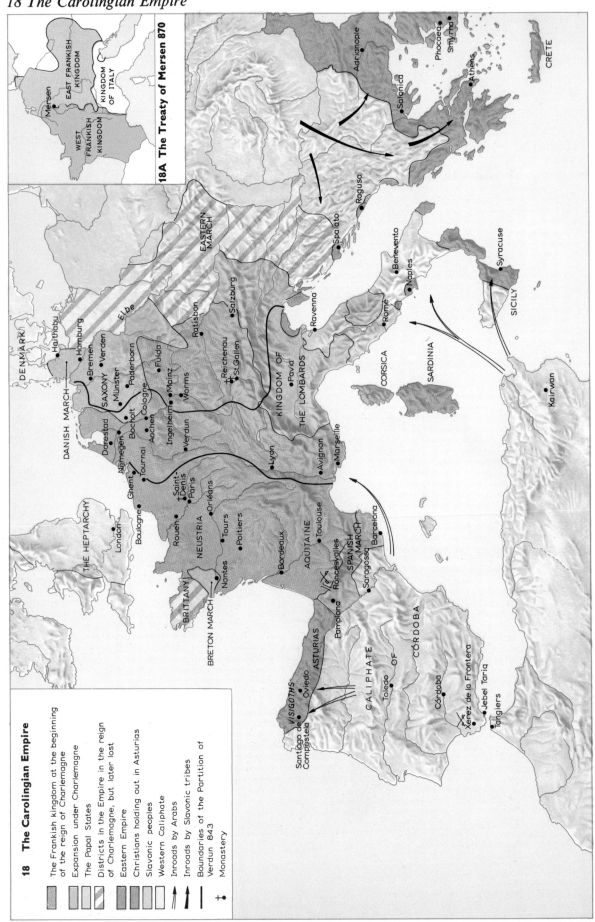

EAST FRANKISH KINGDOM

KINGDOM OF ITALY

WEST FRANKISH KINGDOM

Mersen

CRETE

Smyrna
Phocaea
Athens
Adrianople
Salonica

Ragusa
Spalato

Benevento
Naples
Ravenna
Rome
Syracuse
SICILY

CORSICA
SARDINIA
Kairwan

EASTERN MARCH

Elbe

DENMARK
Haithabu
Hamburg
Bremen
Verden
SAXONY
Münster
Paderborn
Fulda
Ratisbon
Salzburg
Reichenau
St. Gallen
Worms
Mainz
Ingelheim
Cologne
Bocholt
Dorestad
Nijmegen
Aachen
Verdun
Ghent
Tournai
Saint-Denis
Paris
Orléans
Pavia
Lyon
Avignon
Marseille

DANISH MARCH

KINGDOM OF THE LOMBARDS

THE HEPTARCHY
London
Boulogne
Rouen
Tours
Poitiers
Bordeaux

NEUSTRIA
Nantes
BRITTANY
BRETON MARCH

AQUITAINE
Toulouse
Roncesvalles
Pamplona
SPANISH MARCH
Saragossa
Barcelona

ASTURIAS
VISIGOTHS
Oviedo
Santiago de Compostela

CALIPHATE OF CÓRDOBA
Toledo
Córdoba
Xerez de la Frontera
Jebel Tariq
Tangiers

18   The Carolingian Empire

The Frankish kingdom at the beginning of the reign of Charlemagne

Expansion under Charlemagne

The Papal States

Districts in the Empire in the reign of Charlemagne, but later lost

Eastern Empire

Christians holding out in Asturias

Slavonic peoples

Western Caliphate

Inroads by Arabs

Inroads by Slavonic tribes

Boundaries of the Partition of Verdun 843

Monastery

Indus

Kabul

Kandahar

Samarkand

Bokhara

KHWARIZM

Merv

Nishapur

(KINGDOM OF THE SASSANIDS)

CALIPHATE OF

BAGHDAD

OMAN

Nihavend

Ispahan

Shiraz

HADRAMAUT

Trebizond

ARMENIA

Edessa

Mosul

Baghdad

Ctesiphon

Seleucia

Basra

Kufa

Tigris

Euphrates

Aleppo

SYRIA

Jerusalem

ARABIA

Medina

HEJAZ

Mecca

YEMEN

MAGYARS

KHAZARS

Constantinople

Iconium

CYPRUS

Damascus

PALESTINE

Cairo

Nile

Alexandria

E G Y P T

SLAVS

AVARS

Bari

Salonica

Taranto

KINGDOM
OF THE
LOMBARDS

Rome

Pavia

CORSICA

SARDINIA

SICILY

Kairwan

Tripoli

Carthage

Tours

Poitiers

Narbonne

Roncesvalles

Saragossa

Oviedo

CALIPHATE
OF
CÓRDOBA

Toledo

Córdoba

Sevilla

Granada

Xerez

Tangiers

Jebel Tariq

Morocco

MAGHREB

19 The Conquests of Islam

Islam on the death of Mahomet 632

Expansion to 661

Expansion under the Ommeyads 661–750

Frankish kingdom in the 8th century

Eastern Empire in the 8th century

Asturias

Riga

SAMOGITIA

Memel

LITHUANIA

DENMARK

Haithabu
Oldenburg
Lübeck
Hamburg
POMERANIA
Danzig
PRUSSIA
POMERELIA
Lüneburg
FRIESLAND
Bremen
Thorn
Egmont
HOLLAND
Deventer
SAXONY
Brunswick
BRANDENBURG
Utrecht
Tiel
Münster Hildesheim
Goslar
Magdeburg
POLAND
Quedlinburg
Bruges
Ghent
Merseburg
Liegnitz
Bouvines
LOWER
Cologne
Liège
Meissen
Breslau
LORRAINE
Aachen
MEISSEN
SILESIA
Andernach THURINGIA
Frankfurt
Prague
Ingelheim
Mainz
FRANCONIA
MORAVIA
Trier
Worms
Bamberg
BOHEMIA
FRANCE
Verdun UPPER
Speier
Ratisbon
Metz
Waiblingen
LORRAINE
AUSTRIA
Toul
Staufen
Vienna
Strasbourg
Augsburg
Passau
SWABIA
Gran
Citeaux
Reichenau
Benediktbeuren
Constance St. Gallen
Salzburg
BAVARIA
CARINTHIA
KINGDOM
OF
HUNGARY
ARLES
Matoja Pass
Brenner Pass
Cluny
Lyon
MARCH OF VERONA
la Grande
Legnano
Chartreuse
LOMBARDY Milan
Verona
Pavia
Venice
Belgrade
CROATIA
Piacenza
Arles
Genoa Canossa
Ravenna
KINGDOM
ROMAGNA
OF
ITALY
SERBIA
TUSCANY
CORSICA
Rome
EPIRUS
Thessalonica
Benevento Lucera
Naples APULIA
Amalfi Castel del
Salerno Monte
SARDINIA
CALABRIA
Crotone
Palermo
SICILY

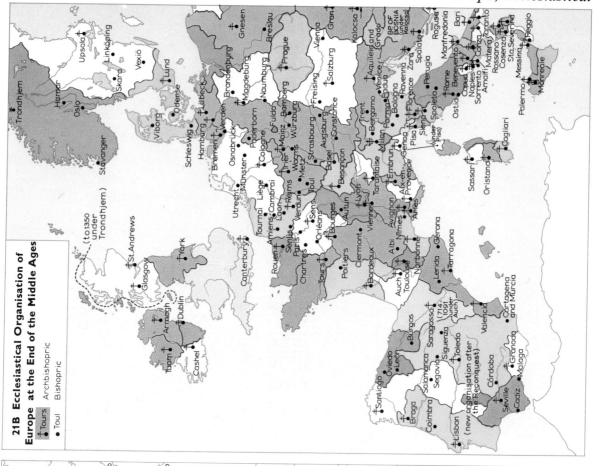

21B Ecclesiastical Organisation of Europe at the End of the Middle Ages

† Tours Archbishopric
• Toul Bishopric

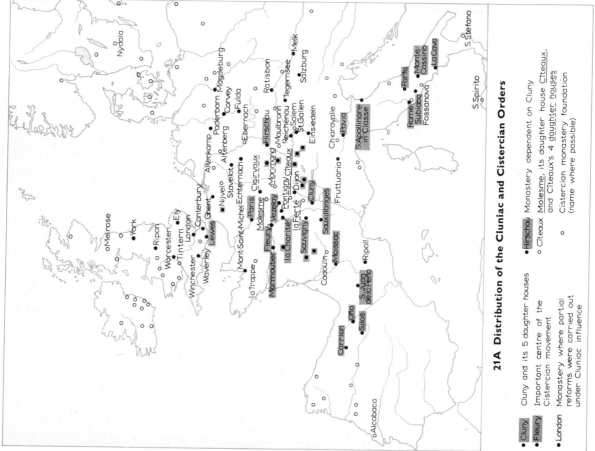

21A Distribution of the Cluniac and Cistercian Orders

Cluny Cluny and its 5 daughter houses

Fleury Important centre of the Cistercian movement

●London Monastery where partial reforms were carried out under Cluniac influence

● Hirschau Monastery dependent on Cluny

○ Citeaux Molesme, its daughter house Cîteaux, and Cîteaux's 4 daughter houses

○ Cistercian monastery foundation (name where possible)

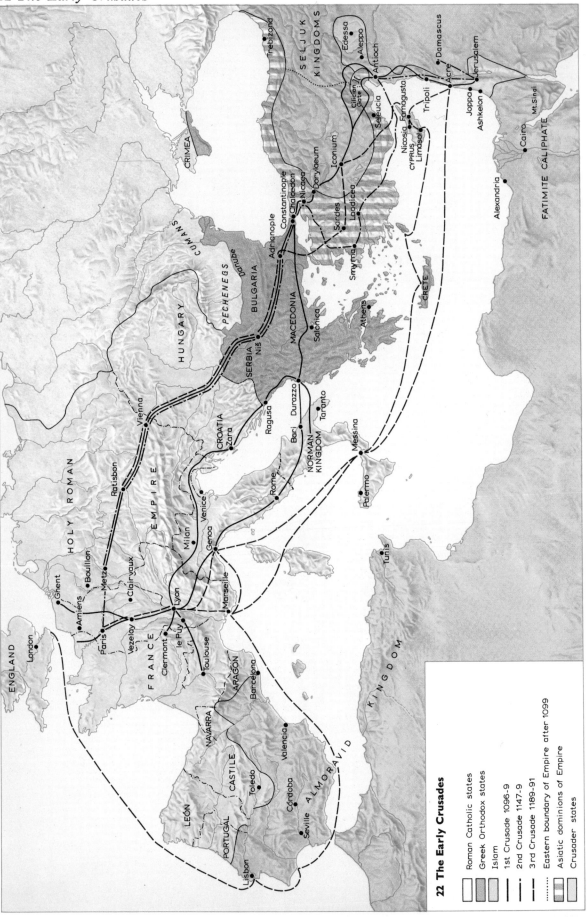

22 The Early Crusades

Roman Catholic states
Greek Orthodox states
Islam
1st Crusade 1096-9
2nd Crusade 1147-9
3rd Crusade 1189-91
Eastern boundary of Empire after 1099
Asiatic dominions of Empire
Crusader states

SELJUK KINGDOM
FATIMITE CALIPHATE
CRIMEA
CUMANS
PECHENEGS
HUNGARY
BULGARIA
MACEDONIA
SERBIA
CROATIA
NORMAN KINGDOM
HOLY ROMAN EMPIRE
FRANCE
ENGLAND
ARAGON
NAVARRA
CASTILE
LEÓN
PORTUGAL
ALMORAVID KINGDOM

Trebizond
Edessa
Aleppo
Antioch
Damascus
Jerusalem
Acre
Seleucia
Cilician Gate
Tripoli
Joppa
Ashkelon
Nicosia Famagusta
CYPRUS Limosol
Mt.Sinai
Cairo
Alexandria
Dorylaeum
Iconium
Nicaea
Chalcedon
Constantinople
Sardes
Laodicea
Smyrna
Athens
CRETE
Salonica
Adrianople
Niš
Danube
Ragusa
Durazzo
Zara
Bari
Taranto
Messina
Palermo
Tunis
Rome
Venice
Genoa
Milan
Vienna
Ratisbon
Metz
Bouillon
Clairvaux
Ghent
Amiens
London
Paris
Vézelay
Lyon
le Puy
Clermont
Marseille
Toulouse
Barcelona
Valencia
Toledo
Córdoba
Seville
Lisbon

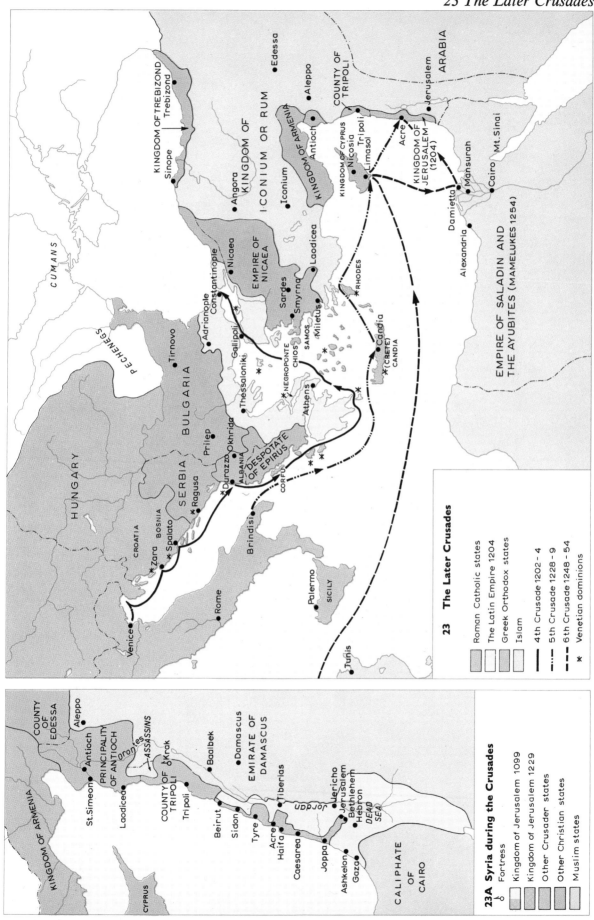

CUMANS

PECHENEGS

KINGDOM OF TREBIZOND
Trebizond
Sinope

KINGDOM OF ICONIUM OR RUM

Edessa
Aleppo
COUNTY OF TRIPOLI
Jerusalem
ARABIA

Angora
KINGDOM OF
Iconium

KINGDOM OF ARMENIA
Antioch
KINGDOM OF CYPRUS
Nicosia
Tripoli
Limasol
Acre
KINGDOM OF JERUSALEM (1204)
Mansurah
Cairo   Mt. Sinai
Damietta
Alexandria

HUNGARY

Tirnovo

SERBIA
BULGARIA

Prilep
Adrianople
Constantinople
Nicaea
EMPIRE OF NICAEA
Sardes
Smyrna
Laodicea

CROATIA
Zara
BOSNIA
Spalato
Ragusa
Durazzo
Okhrida
ALBANIA
DESPOTE OF EPIRUS
Thessaloniki
NEGROPONTE
CHIOS
SAMOS
Miletus
RHODES
Candia
(CRETE)
CANDIA

Rome

Brindisi

Venice
CORFU
Athens

Palermo
SICILY

Tunis

EMPIRE OF SALADIN AND THE AYUBITES (MAMELUKES 1254)

23A Syria during the Crusades

COUNTY OF EDESSA
Aleppo
Antioch
St. Simeon
PRINCIPALITY OF ANTIOCH
ASSASSINS
Orontes
Krak
Laodicea
Baalbek
Damascus
EMIRATE OF DAMASCUS
COUNTY OF TRIPOLI
Tripoli
Beirut
Sidon
Tyre
Acre
Haifa
Caesarea
Tiberias
Jordan
Jericho
Jerusalem
Bethlehem
Hebron
DEAD SEA
Joppa
Ashkelon
Gaza
CALIPHATE OF CAIRO

KINGDOM OF ARMENIA

CYPRUS

Kingdom of Jerusalem 1099	
Kingdom of Jerusalem 1229	
Other Crusader states	
Other Christian states	
Muslim states	

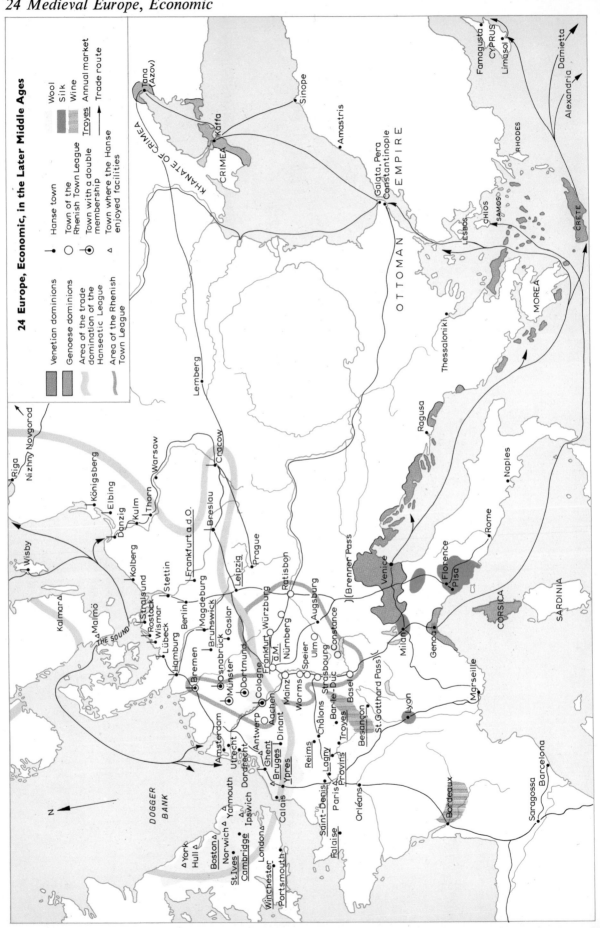

24 Europe, Economic, in the Later Middle Ages

- • Hanse town
- ○ Town of the Rhenish Town League
- ⊙ Town with a double membership
- △ Town where the Hanse enjoyed facilities

Wool
Silk
Wine
<u>Troyes</u> Annual market
→ Trade route

Venetian dominions
Genoese dominions
Area of the trade domination of the Hanseatic League
Area of the Rhenish Town League

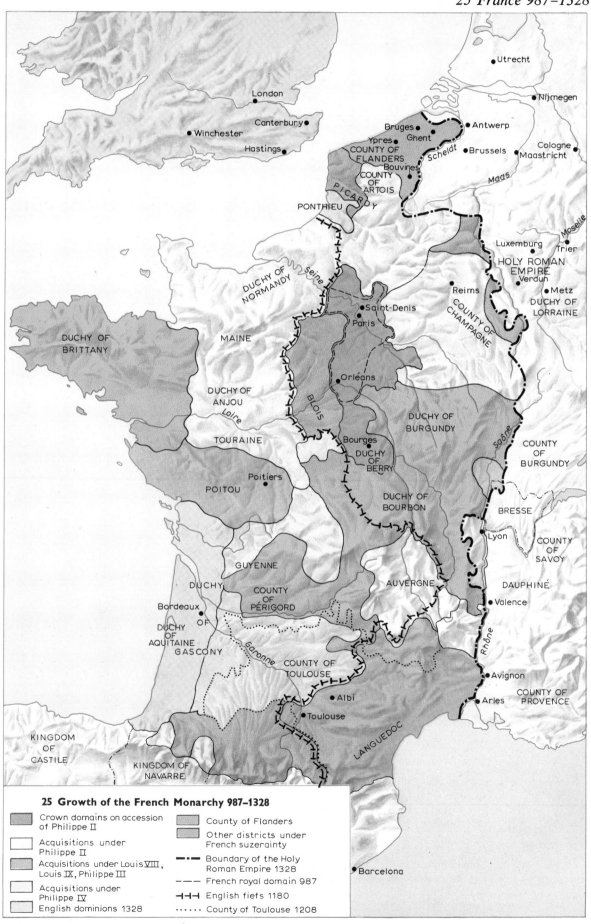

Utrecht

Nijmegen

London

Canterbury

Winchester

Hastings

Bruges
Ghent
Antwerp

Ypres
COUNTY OF
FLANDERS
Bouvines
COUNTY OF
ARTOIS

Brussels

Cologne
Maastricht

Scheldt

Maas

PICARDY

PONTHIEU

Luxemburg
Trier

Moselle

HOLY ROMAN
EMPIRE
Verdun

Metz
DUCHY OF
LORRAINE

DUCHY OF
NORMANDY

Seine

Reims

Saint-Denis
Paris

COUNTY
OF
CHAMPAGNE

DUCHY OF
BRITTANY

MAINE

DUCHY OF
ANJOU

Loire

Orléans

BLOIS

TOURAINE

Bourges
DUCHY
OF
BERRY

DUCHY OF
BURGUNDY

Saône

COUNTY
OF
BURGUNDY

POITOU

Poitiers

DUCHY OF
BOURBON

BRESSE

Lyon

COUNTY
OF
SAVOY

GUYENNE

DUCHY

Bordeaux
OF

DUCHY
OF
AQUITAINE
GASCONY

COUNTY
OF
PÉRIGORD

AUVERGNE

DAUPHINÉ

Valence

COUNTY OF
TOULOUSE

Albi

Toulouse

LANGUEDOC

Avignon

Arles

COUNTY OF
PROVENCE

Rhône

Garonne

KINGDOM
OF
CASTILE

KINGDOM OF
NAVARRE

Barcelona

25 Growth of the French Monarchy 987–1328

- Crown domains on accession of Philippe II
- Acquisitions under Philippe II
- Acquisitions under Louis VIII, Louis IX, Philippe III
- Acquisitions under Philippe IV
- English dominions 1328
- County of Flanders
- Other districts under French suzerainty
- ·–··– Boundary of the Holy Roman Empire 1328
- – – – French royal domain 987
- ⊢+⊣ English fiefs 1180
- ······ County of Toulouse 1208

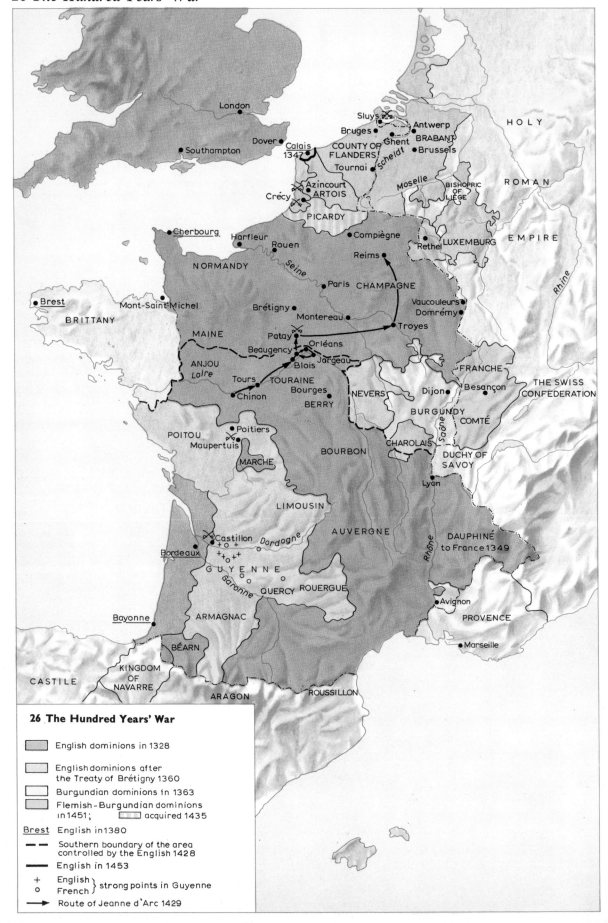

London

Dover

Southampton

Calais
1347

Sluys

Bruges

Antwerp

Ghent

BRABANT

Brussels

COUNTY OF
FLANDERS

Tournai

Scheldt

Moselle

BISHOPRIC
OF
LIÈGE

Azincourt

ARTOIS

Crécy

PICARDY

HOLY

ROMAN

EMPIRE

Cherbourg

Harfleur

Rouen

Compiègne

Rethel

LUXEMBURG

Reims

NORMANDY

Seine

Paris

CHAMPAGNE

Brest

Mont-Saint-Michel

Brétigny

Montereau

Vaucouleurs

Domrémy

BRITTANY

MAINE

Patay

Orléans

Beaugency

Jargeau

Troyes

Rhine

ANJOU

Loire

Blois

Tours

TOURAINE

Bourges

BERRY

NEVERS

Chinon

FRANCHE

Dijon

Besançon

THE SWISS
CONFEDERATION

BURGUNDY

COMTÉ

Poitiers

POITOU

Maupertuis

MARCHE

BOURBON

CHAROLAIS

Saône

DUCHY OF
SAVOY

Lyon

LIMOUSIN

AUVERGNE

Castillon

Dordogne

DAUPHINÉ
to France 1349

Bordeaux

GUYENNE

Garonne

QUERCY

ROUERGUE

Rhône

Avignon

PROVENCE

Bayonne

ARMAGNAC

BÉARN

Marseille

CASTILE

KINGDOM
OF
NAVARRE

ARAGON

ROUSSILLON

26 The Hundred Years' War

English dominions in 1328

English dominions after
the Treaty of Brétigny 1360

Burgundian dominions in 1363

Flemish–Burgundian dominions
in 1451; acquired 1435

Brest English in 1380

- - - Southern boundary of the area
controlled by the English 1428

English in 1453

+ English }
o French } strong points in Guyenne

→ Route of Jeanne d'Arc 1429

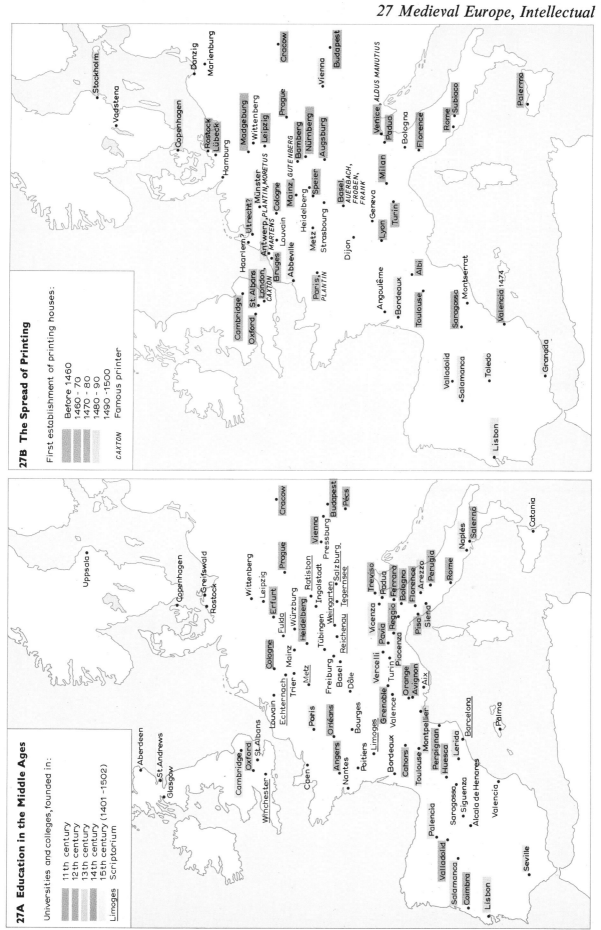

27A Education in the Middle Ages

Universities and colleges, founded in:

11th century
12th century
13th century
14th century
15th century (1401-1502)

Limoges   Scriptorium

27B The Spread of Printing

First establishment of printing houses:

Before 1460
1460 - 70
1470 - 80
1480 - 90
1490 -1500

CAXTON   Famous printer

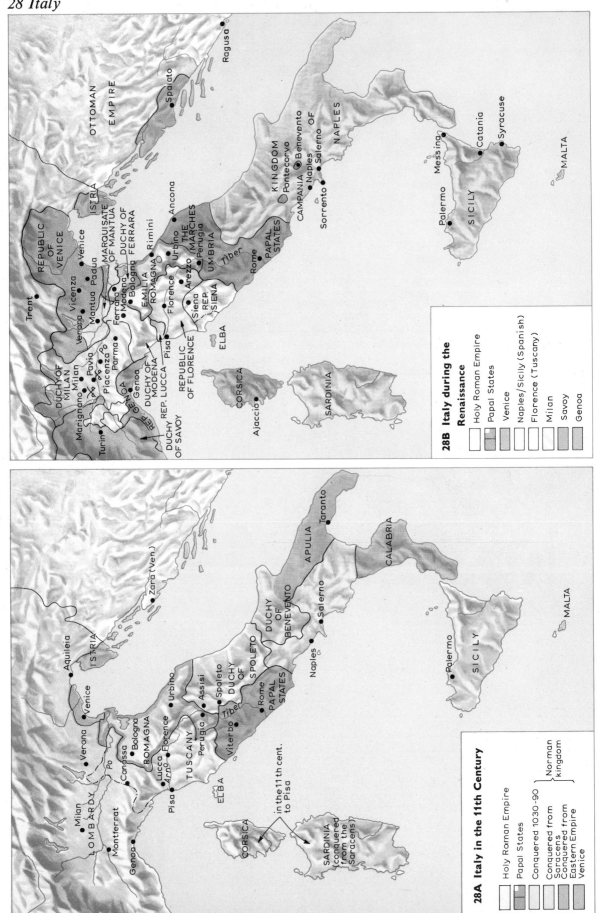

28B Italy during the Renaissance

OTTOMAN EMPIRE

Spalato
Ragusa

REPUBLIC OF VENICE

ISTRIA
Venice
Padua
Vicenza
MARQUISATE OF MANTUA
DUCHY OF FERRARA
Mantua
Verona
Trent
Po
DUCHY OF MILAN
Milan
Pavia
Piacenza
Parma
Marignano
Turin
REP. OF GENOA
Genoa
DUCHY OF MODENA
REP. LUCCA
REPUBLIC OF FLORENCE
DUCHY OF SAVOY
Ferrara
Modena
Bologna
EMILIA
ROMAGNA
Florence
Pisa
Lucca
Arezzo
UMBRIA
Perugia
Urbino
THE MARCHES
Rimini
Ancona
REP. SIENA
Siena
Tiber
Rome
PAPAL STATES
ELBA
CORSICA
Ajaccio
SARDINIA

KINGDOM OF NAPLES
Pontecorvo
Benevento
CAMPANIA
Naples
Salerno
Sorrento

Messina
Palermo
SICILY
Catania
Syracuse
MALTA

Legend:
Holy Roman Empire
Papal States
Venice
Naples/Sicily (Spanish)
Florence (Tuscany)
Milan
Savoy
Genoa

28A Italy in the 11th Century

Aquileia
ISTRIA
Venice
Zara (Ven.)
Verona
LOMBARDY
Milan
Montferrat
Genoa
Po
Canossa
Bologna
ROMAGNA
Lucca
Arno
Pisa
Florence
TUSCANY
Perugia
Urbino
Assisi
Spoleto
DUCHY OF SPOLETO
Viterbo
Tiber
Rome
PAPAL STATES
DUCHY OF BENEVENTO
Benevento
Salerno
Naples
APULIA
Taranto
CALABRIA
ELBA
CORSICA
SARDINIA (conquered from the Saracens)
in the 11th cent. to Pisa
MALTA
Palermo
SICILY

Legend:
Holy Roman Empire
Papal States
Conquered 1030-90
Conquered from Saracens   } Norman kingdom
Conquered from Eastern Empire
Venice

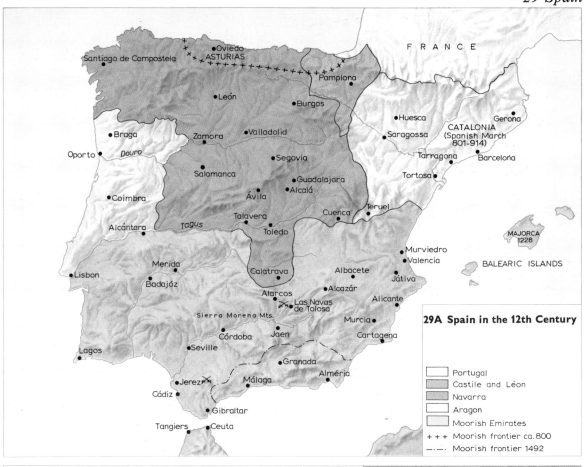

29A Spain in the 12th Century

Portugal
Castile and Léon
Navarra
Aragon
Moorish Emirates
+ + + Moorish frontier ca.800
–·–·– Moorish frontier 1492

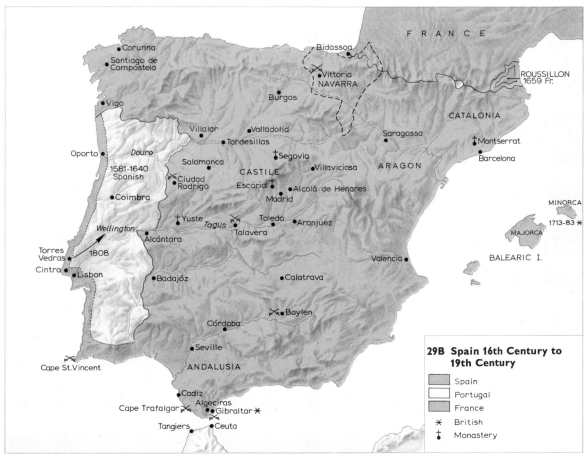

29B Spain 16th Century to 19th Century

Spain
Portugal
France
✳ British
✝ Monastery

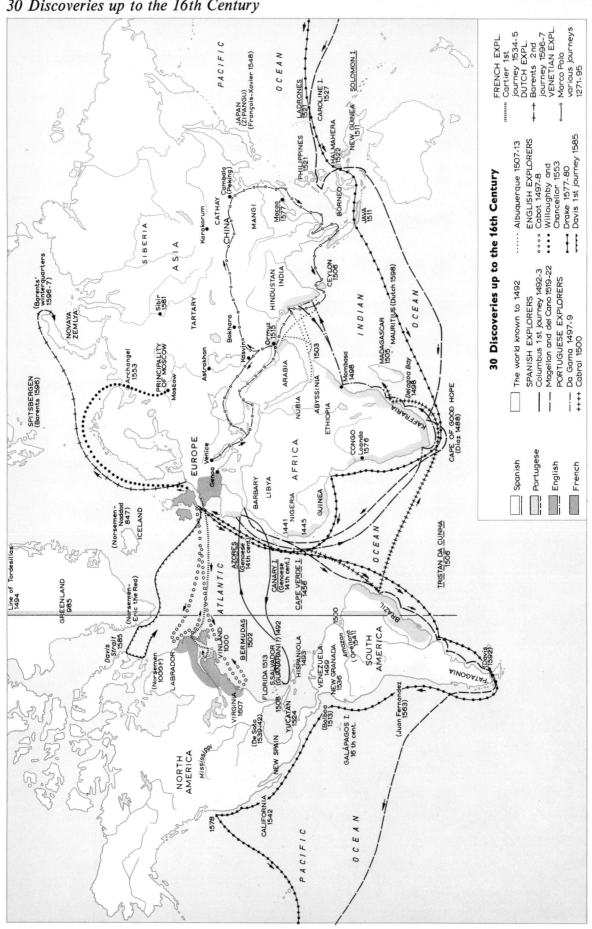

30 Discoveries up to the 16th Century

	The world known to 1492			Albuquerque 1507-13	FRENCH EXPL.
					Cartier 1st journey 1534-5

SPANISH EXPLORERS
Columbus 1st journey 1492-3
Magellan and del Cano 1519-22

PORTUGUESE EXPLORERS
Da Gama 1497-9
Cabral 1500

ENGLISH EXPLORERS
Cabot 1497-8
Willoughby and Chancellor 1553
Drake 1577-80
Davis 1st journey 1585

FRENCH EXPL.
Cartier 1st journey 1534-5

DUTCH EXPL.
Barents 2nd journey 1596-7

VENETIAN EXPL.
Marco Polo various journeys 1271-95

Spanish
Portugese
English
French

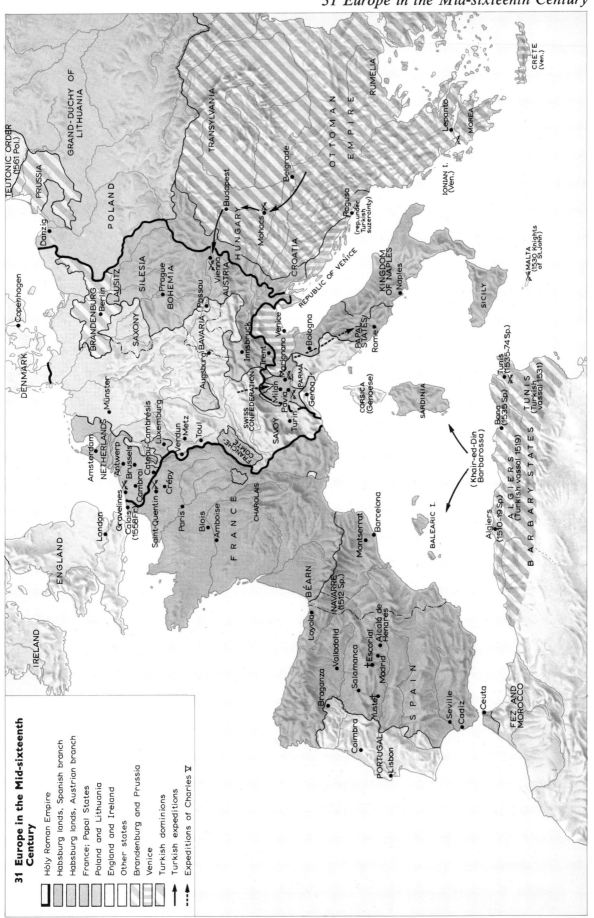

Holy Roman Empire
Habsburg lands, Spanish branch
Habsburg lands, Austrian branch
France; Papal States
Poland and Lithuania
England and Ireland
Other states
Brandenburg and Prussia
Venice
Turkish dominions
Turkish expeditions
Expeditions of Charles V

CRETE (Ven.)

TEUTONIC ORDER (1561 Pol.)
PRUSSIA
GRAND-DUCHY OF LITHUANIA
Danzig
POLAND
TRANSYLVANIA
OTTOMAN EMPIRE
RUMELIA
Lepanto
MOREA
Belgrade
Budapest
Mohács
Copenhagen
DENMARK
BRANDENBURG
Berlin
LAUSITZ
SILESIA
SAXONY
Prague
BOHEMIA
BAVARIA
Augsburg
Passau
Vienna
AUSTRIA
HUNGARY
CROATIA
Ragusa (rep. under Turkish suzerainty)
IONIAN I. (Ven.)
MALTA (1530 Knights of St John)
Münster
Innsbruck
Trent
Venice
Marignano
Bologna
PAPAL STATES
Rome
KINGDOM OF NAPLES
Naples
SICILY
REPUBLIC OF VENICE
Amsterdam
NETHERLANDS
Antwerp
Brussels
Cateau-Cambrésis
Luxemburg
Verdun
Metz
Toul
SWISS CONFEDERATION
Milan
Pavia
SAVOY
Turin
Genoa
PARMA
FRANCHE-COMTÉ
CORSICA (Genoese)
SARDINIA
Bona
TUNIS (1535 Sp.)
Tunis (1535-74 Sp.)
TUNIS (Turkish vassal 1531)
London
Cambrai
Crépy
Saint-Quentin
Gravelines
Calais (1558 Fr.)
CHAROLAIS
Paris
Blois
Amboise
FRANCE
(Khair-ed-Din Barbarossa)
ENGLAND
IRELAND
Barcelona
Montserrat
BALEARIC I.
ALGIERS (Turkish vassal 1519)
Algiers (1510-19 Sp.)
BARBARY STATES
BÉARN
NAVARRE (1512 Sp.)
Loyola
Valladolid
Salamanca
Escorial
Madrid
Alcalá de Henares
SPAIN
Seville
Cadiz
Ceuta
Braganza
Coimbra
Mustel
PORTUGAL
Lisbon
FEZ AND MOROCCO

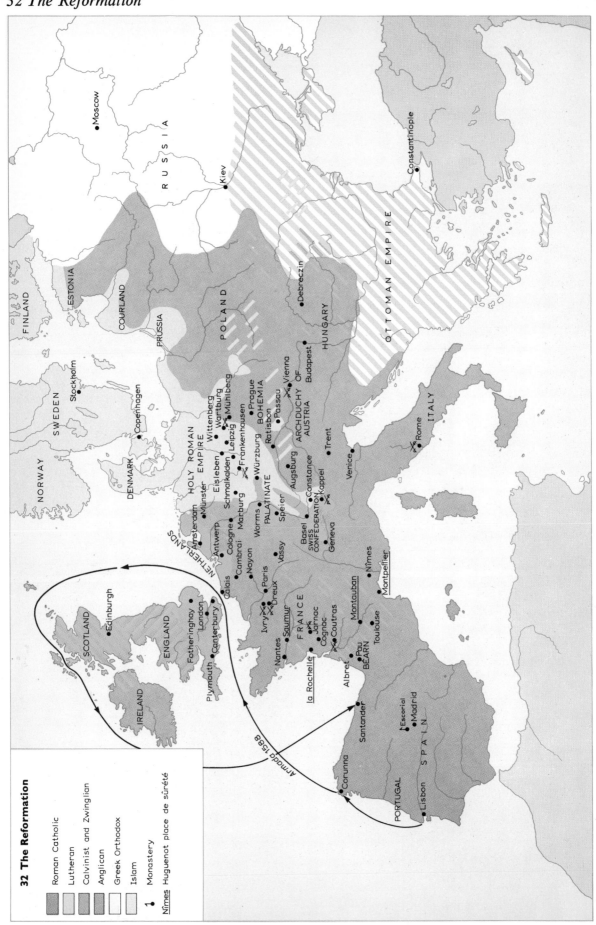

32 The Reformation

- Roman Catholic
- Lutheran
- Calvinist and Zwinglian
- Anglican
- Greek Orthodox
- Islam
- Monastery

Nîmes Huguenot place de sûreté

RUSSIA

Moscow

Kiev

FINLAND

ESTONIA

COURLAND

PRUSSIA

SWEDEN

Stockholm

NORWAY

DENMARK

Copenhagen

POLAND

HUNGARY

Debreczin

Budapest

OTTOMAN EMPIRE

Constantinople

HOLY ROMAN EMPIRE

Wittenberg

Wartburg

Mühlberg

Eisleben

Leipzig

Schmalkalden

Frankenhausen

Prague

BOHEMIA

Würzburg

Ratisbon

Passau

Vienna

ARCHDUCHY OF AUSTRIA

Trent

Venice

Rome

ITALY

Münster

Amsterdam

Antwerp

Cologne

Marburg

Worms

PALATINATE

Speier

Augsburg

Constance

Basel

SWISS CONFEDERATION

Geneva

Kappel

NETHERLANDS

Calais

Cambrai

Noyon

Paris

Dreux

Vassy

Nîmes

Montpelier

Montauban

SCOTLAND

Edinburgh

ENGLAND

Fotheringhay

London

Canterbury

Plymouth

IRELAND

Nantes

Ivry

Saumur

FRANCE

Jarnac

Cognac

Coutras

la Rochelle

Albret

Pau

BEARN

Toulouse

Santander

Escorial

Madrid

SPAIN

Corunna

Lisbon

PORTUGAL

Armada 1588

33 The Thirty Years' War 1618–48

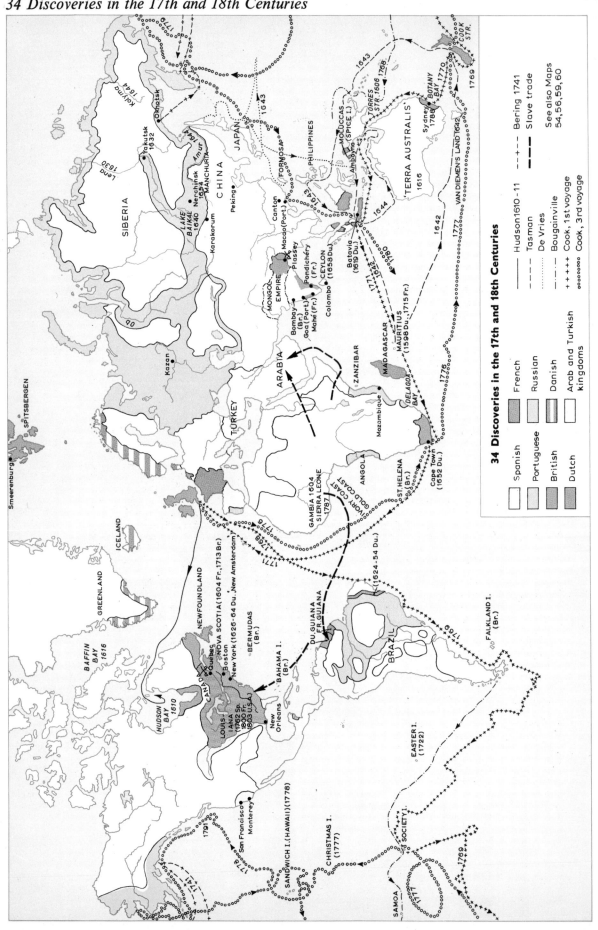

34 Discoveries in the 17th and 18th Centuries

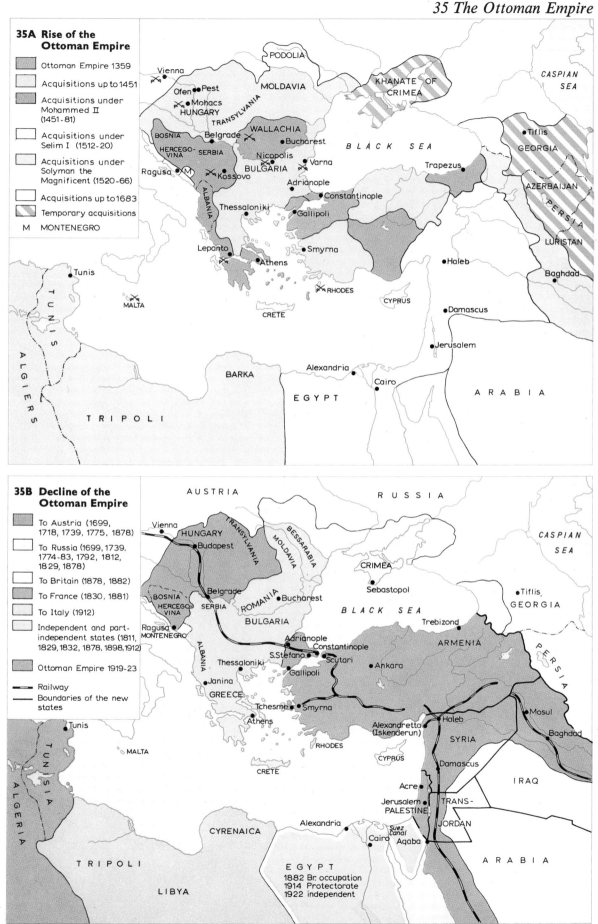

35A Rise of the Ottoman Empire

Ottoman Empire 1359

Acquisitions up to 1451

Acquisitions under Mohammed II (1451-81)

Acquisitions under Selim I (1512-20)

Acquisitions under Solyman the Magnificent (1520-66)

Acquisitions up to 1683

Temporary acquisitions

M   MONTENEGRO

PODOLIA

Vienna

KHANATE OF CRIMEA

CASPIAN SEA

Ofen • Pest
• Mohacs
HUNGARY

MOLDAVIA

TRANSYLVANIA

BOSNIA

Belgrade

WALLACHIA

Bucharest

BLACK SEA

• Tiflis

GEORGIA

HERCEGO-VINA   SERBIA

Nicopolis

Varna

Trapezus

AZERBAIJAN

Ragusa • M

Kossovo

BULGARIA

Adrianople

ALBANIA

Thessaloniki

Constantinople

Gallipoli

PERSIA

LURISTAN

Lepanto

Athens

• Smyrna

• Haleb

Baghdad

• Tunis

MALTA

RHODES

CYPRUS

• Damascus

CRETE

• Jerusalem

TUNIS

ALGIERS

BARKA

Alexandria

EGYPT

Cairo

ARABIA

TRIPOLI

35B Decline of the Ottoman Empire

To Austria (1699, 1718, 1739, 1775, 1878)

To Russia (1699, 1739, 1774-83, 1792, 1812, 1829, 1878)

To Britain (1878, 1882)

To France (1830, 1881)

To Italy (1912)

Independent and part-independent states (1811, 1829, 1832, 1878, 1898, 1912)

Ottoman Empire 1919-23

━━ Railway

━━ Boundaries of the new states

AUSTRIA

RUSSIA

Vienna

HUNGARY

Budapest

TRANSYLVANIA

BESSARABIA

MOLDAVIA

CRIMEA

CASPIAN SEA

Belgrade

BOSNIA
HERCEGO-VINA

SERBIA

ROMANIA

Bucharest

Sebastopol

• Tiflis

GEORGIA

Ragusa

MONTENEGRO

BULGARIA

BLACK SEA

Trebizond

ALBANIA

Thessaloniki

Adrianople

S.Stefano

Constantinople

Scutari

ARMENIA

PERSIA

Janina

Gallipoli

• Ankara

GREECE

Tchesme • Smyrna

Athens

Alexandretta
(Iskenderun)

Haleb

Mosul

RHODES

SYRIA

Baghdad

• Tunis

MALTA

CYPRUS

CRETE

Damascus

IRAQ

TUNISIA

Acre

ALGERIA

Jerusalem
PALESTINE

TRANS-
JORDAN

Aqaba

CYRENAICA

Alexandria

Suez
Canal

Cairo

ARABIA

TRIPOLI

EGYPT
1882 Br. occupation
1914 Protectorate
1922 independent

LIBYA

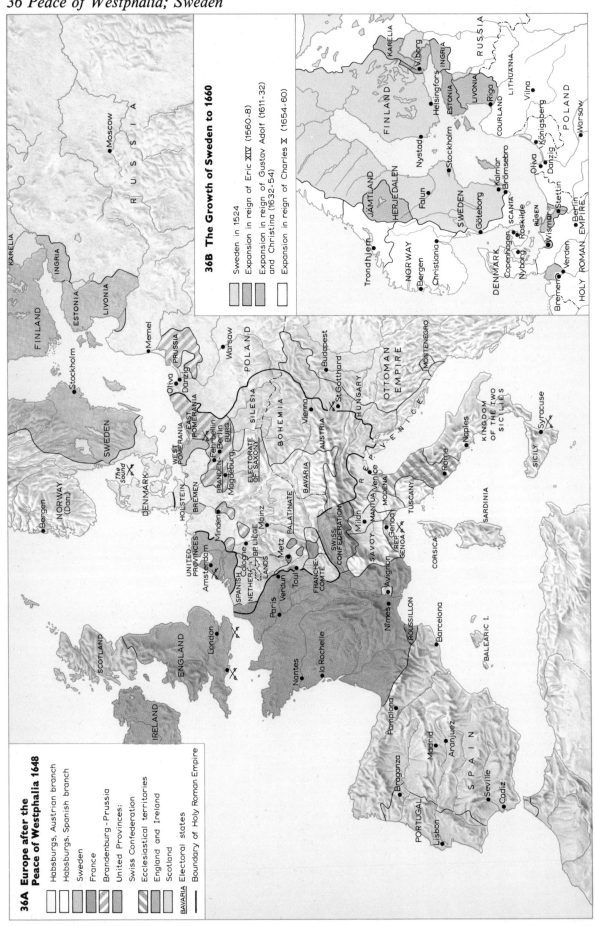

36A Europe after the Peace of Westphalia 1648

Habsburgs, Austrian branch
Habsburgs, Spanish branch
Sweden
France
Brandenburg–Prussia
United Provinces;
Swiss Confederation
Ecclesiastical territories
England and Ireland
Scotland
BAVARIA Electoral states
—— Boundary of Holy Roman Empire

36B The Growth of Sweden to 1660

Sweden in 1524
Expansion in reign of Eric XIV (1560–8)
Expansion in reign of Gustav Adolf (1611–32)
and Christina (1632–54)
Expansion in reign of Charles X (1654–60)

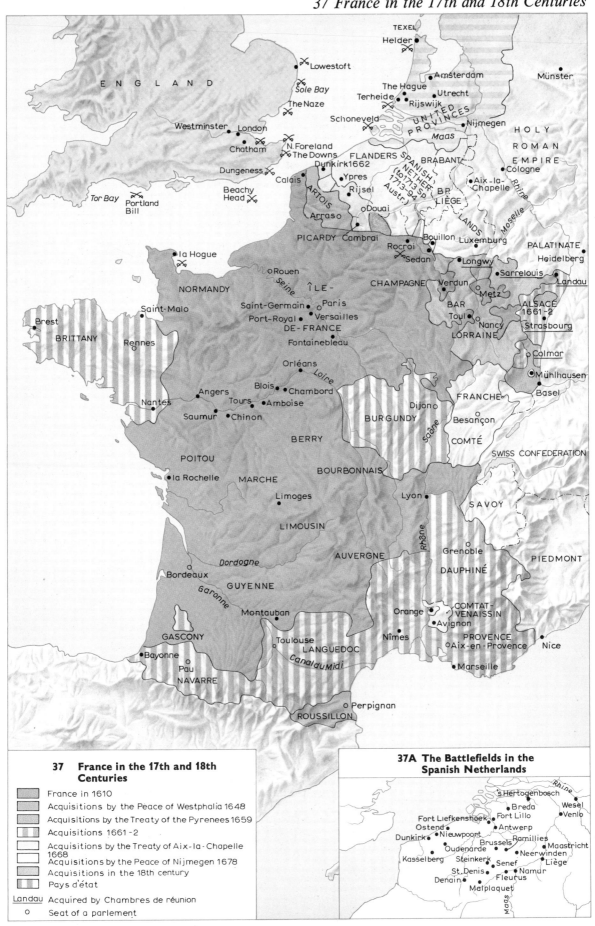

TEXEL
Helder
Lowestoft
Sole Bay
The Naze
Amsterdam
Münster
E N G L A N D
The Hague
Utrecht
Terheide
Rijswijk
Schoneveld
UNITED
Nijmegen
HOLY
Westminster
London
PROVINCES
ROMAN
Chatham
N. Foreland
Maas
EMPIRE
The Downs
FLANDERS
SPANISH
BRABANT
Dungeness
Dunkirk 1662
NETHER.
Aix-la-
Cologne
Tor Bay
Beachy
Ypres
(to 1713 SP.
Chapelle
Portland
Head
Calais
Rijsel
1713-94
Rhine
Bill
ARTOIS
oDouai
Austr.)
LIÈGE
Arraso
LANDS
Moselle
la Hogue
PICARDY
Cambrai
Rocroi
Bouillon
Luxemburg
PALATINATE
Sedan
Longwy
Heidelberg
NORMANDY
Seine
ÎLE-
CHAMPAGNE
Verdun
Sarrelouis
Landau
oRouen
Metz
ALSACE
Saint-Germain
Paris
BAR
1661-2
Port-Royal
Versailles
Toul
Strasbourg
DE-FRANCE
Nancy
Fontainebleau
LORRAINE
Colmar
Orléans
Loire
FRANCHE
Mühlhausen
Saint-Malo
Blois
Chambord
Dijono
Basel
Brest
Angers
Tours
Amboise
Besançon
BRITTANY
Saumur
Chinon
BURGUNDY
COMTÉ
Rennes
Saône
SWISS CONFEDERATION
Nantes
BERRY
POITOU
BOURBONNAIS
SAVOY
la Rochelle
MARCHE
Lyon
Limoges
PIEDMONT
LIMOUSIN
Rhône
Grenoble
Dordogne
AUVERGNE
DAUPHINÉ
Bordeaux
GUYENNE
Garonne
COMTAT-
Orange
VENAISSIN
Montauban
Avignon
Nice
Toulouse
Nîmes
PROVENCE
GASCONY
LANGUEDOC
Aix-en-Provence
Bayonne
Canal du Midi
Marseille
Pau
NAVARRE
Perpignan
ROUSSILLON

**37A The Battlefields in the
      Spanish Netherlands**

Rhine
's Hertogenbosch
Wesel
Breda
Fort Lillo
Venlo
Fort Liefkenshoek
Antwerp
Ostend
Nieuwpoort
Ramillies
Dunkirk
Brussels
Maastricht
Oudenarde
Neerwinden
Kasselberg
Steinkerk
Senef
Liège
St. Denis
Namur
Denain
Fleurus
Malplaquet
Maas

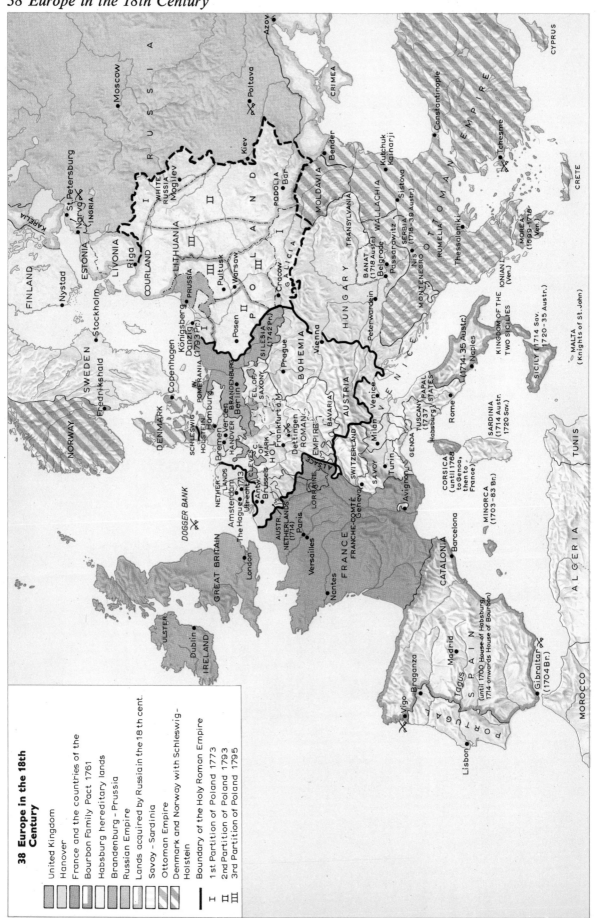

38 Europe in the 18th Century

- United Kingdom
- Hanover
- France and the countries of the
- Bourbon Family Pact 1761
- Habsburg hereditary lands
- Brandenburg – Prussia
- Russian Empire
- Lands acquired by Russia in the 18th cent.
- Savoy – Sardinia
- Ottoman Empire
- Denmark and Norway with Schleswig-Holstein
- Boundary of the Holy Roman Empire

I   1st Partition of Poland 1773
II 2nd Partition of Poland 1793
III 3rd Partition of Poland 1795

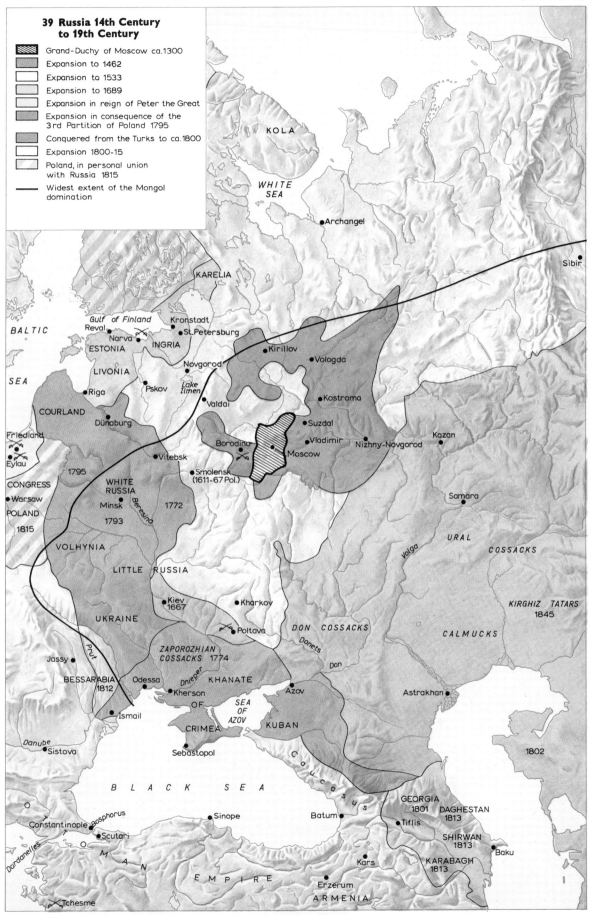

**39 Russia 14th Century
to 19th Century**

Grand-Duchy of Moscow ca.1300
Expansion to 1462
Expansion to 1533
Expansion to 1689
Expansion in reign of Peter the Great
Expansion in consequence of the
3rd Partition of Poland 1795
Conquered from the Turks to ca.1800
Expansion 1800-15
Poland, in personal union
with Russia 1815
Widest extent of the Mongol
domination

KOLA

WHITE
SEA

Archangel

Sibir

KARELIA

BALTIC

Gulf of Finland   Kronstadt
Reval   Narva   St.Petersburg   Kirillov   Vologda
ESTONIA   INGRIA
LIVONIA   Novgorod   Kostroma
Riga   Pskov   Lake   Kazan
Ilmen
COURLAND   Valdai   Suzdal
Dünaburg   Borodino   Vladimir   Nizhny-Novgorod
Friedland   Vitebsk   Moscow
Eylau   1795   Smolensk   Samara
(1611-67 Pol.)
CONGRESS   WHITE
Warsaw   RUSSIA   1772   URAL
POLAND   Minsk   COSSACKS
1815   1793
VOLHYNIA   KIRGHIZ TATARS
LITTLE   RUSSIA   1845
CALMUCKS
UKRAINE   Kiev   Kharkov
1667
Poltava   DON COSSACKS
Jassy   ZAPOROZHIAN   Donets
COSSACKS   1774   Don
BESSARABIA   Odessa   Dnieper   KHANATE
1812   Kherson   Azov   Astrakhan
Ismail   SEA   OF
OF   AZOV   KUBAN
Danube   CRIMEA
Sistova   Sebastopol   Caucasus   1802

BLACK   SEA   GEORGIA   DAGHESTAN
1801   1813
Constantinople   Bosphorus   Sinope   Batum   Tiflis
Scutari   SHIRWAN
Dardanelles   Kars   1813   Baku
KARABAGH
EMPIRE   Erzerum   1813
ARMENIA
Tchesme

SEA

Valdai
Beresina
Volga
Prut

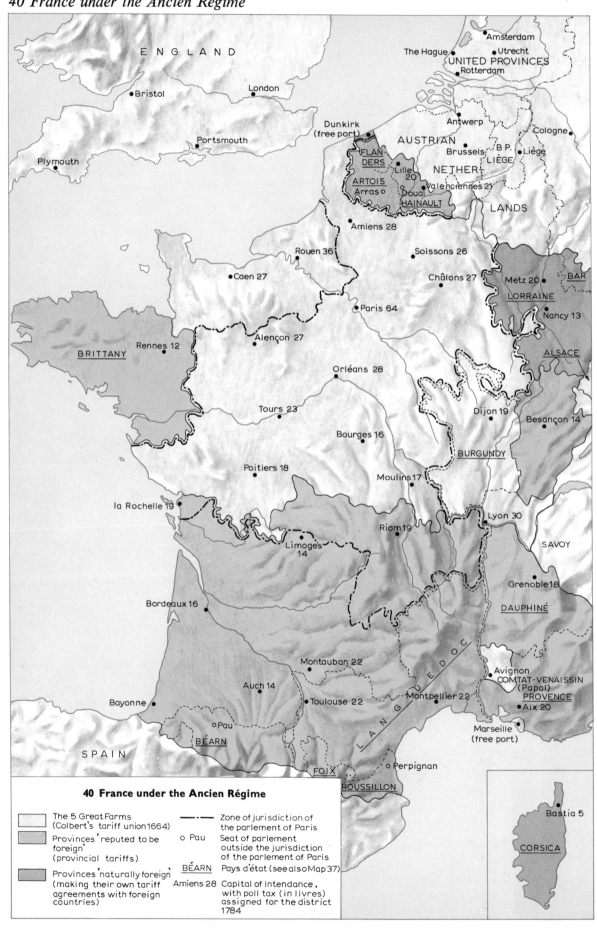

ENGLAND

Amsterdam
Utrecht
The Hague   UNITED PROVINCES
Rotterdam

Bristol
London

Portsmouth

Plymouth

Antwerp   Cologne
Dunkirk   AUSTRIAN   B.P.   Liège
(free port)   Brussels   LIÈGE
FLAN-   Lille   NETHER-
DERS   20
ARTOIS   Valenciennes 21   LANDS
Arras o   Douai
HAINAULT

Amiens 28

Rouen 36   Soissons 26

Caen 27   Châlons 27   Metz 20   BAR
LORRAINE
Paris 64   Nancy 13

Alençon 27   ALSACE

BRITTANY
Rennes 12

Orléans 28

Tours 23   Dijon 19   Besançon 14

Bourges 16   BURGUNDY

Poitiers 18   Moulins 17

la Rochelle 19   Lyon 30
Riom 19   SAVOY
Limoges
14
Grenoble 18

Bordeaux 16   DAUPHINÉ

Montauban 22   Avignon
COMTAT-VENAISSIN
Auch 14   (Papal)
PROVENCE
Bayonne   Toulouse 22   Montpellier 22   Aix 20

o Pau   Marseille
BÉARN   (free port)

SPAIN   o Perpignan
FOIX
ROUSSILLON

Bastia 5

CORSICA

40 France under the Ancien Régime

☐	The 5 Great Farms (Colbert's tariff union 1664)	▬·▬·▬ Zone of jurisdiction of the parlement of Paris
☐	Provinces 'reputed to be foreign' (provincial tariffs)	o Pau Seat of parlement outside the jurisdiction of the parlement of Paris
☐	Provinces 'naturally foreign' (making their own tariff agreements with foreign countries)	BÉARN Pays d'état (see also Map 37)
		Amiens 28 Capital of intendance, with poll tax (in livres) assigned for the district 1784

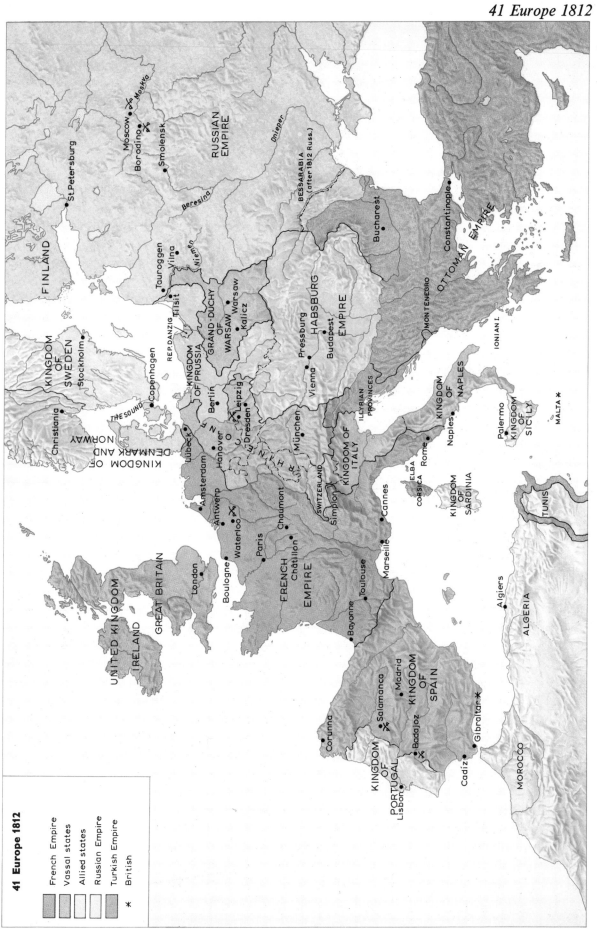

41 Europe 1812

French Empire
Vassal states
Allied states
Russian Empire
Turkish Empire
* British

RUSSIAN EMPIRE

Moscow
Moskwa
Borodino
Smolensk
St. Petersburg
Beresina
BESSARABIA
(after 1812 Russ.)
Bucharest

FINLAND

KINGDOM OF SWEDEN
Stockholm
Christiania
KINGDOM OF DENMARK AND NORWAY
Copenhagen
THE SOUND

Tauroggen
Vilna
Niemen
Tilsit
REP. DANZIG
GRAND-DUCHY OF WARSAW
Warsaw
Kalicz
KINGDOM OF PRUSSIA
Berlin
Lübeck
Hanover
Leipzig
Dresden
Pressburg
Budapest
Vienna
München
HABSBURG EMPIRE

OTTOMAN EMPIRE
Constantinople
MONTENEGRO
IONIAN I.
MALTA *

UNITED KINGDOM
IRELAND
GREAT BRITAIN
London

Amsterdam
Antwerp
Waterloo
Boulogne
Paris
Chaumont
Châtillon
FRENCH EMPIRE
SWITZERLAND
Simplon
Cannes
Marseille
Toulouse
Bayonne
ILLYRIAN PROVINCES
KINGDOM OF ITALY
Rome
ELBA
CORSICA
KINGDOM OF SARDINIA
KINGDOM OF NAPLES
Naples
Palermo
KINGDOM OF SICILY

KINGDOM OF PORTUGAL
Lisbon
Corunna
Salamanca
Madrid
Badajoz
KINGDOM OF SPAIN
Cadiz
Gibraltar *

Algiers
ALGERIA
TUNIS
MOROCCO

Dnieper

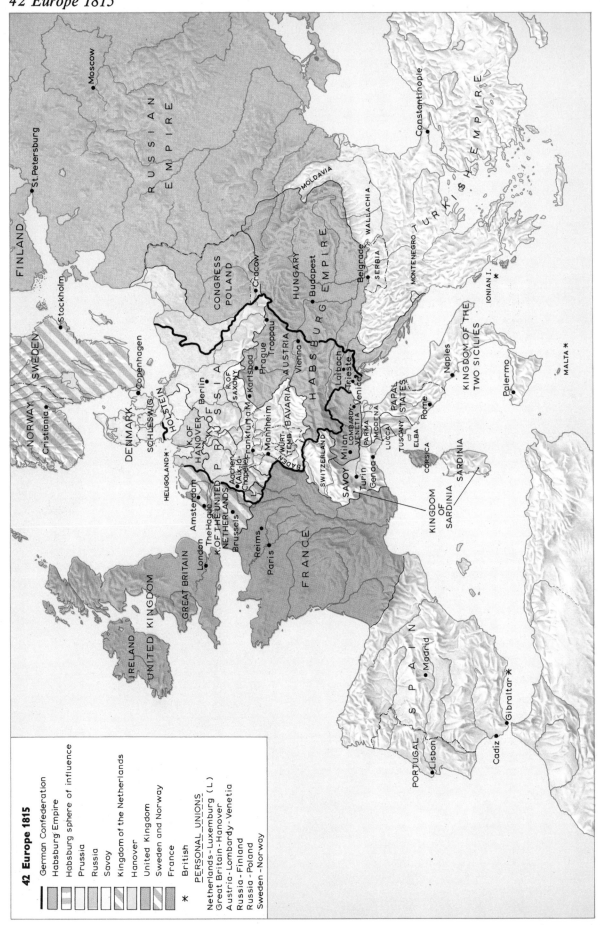

German Confederation
Habsburg Empire
Habsburg sphere of influence
Prussia
Russia
Savoy
Kingdom of the Netherlands
Hanover
United Kingdom
Sweden and Norway
France

* British

PERSONAL UNIONS
Netherlands-Luxemburg (L)
Great Britain-Hanover
Austria-Lombardy-Venetia
Russia-Finland
Russia-Poland
Sweden-Norway

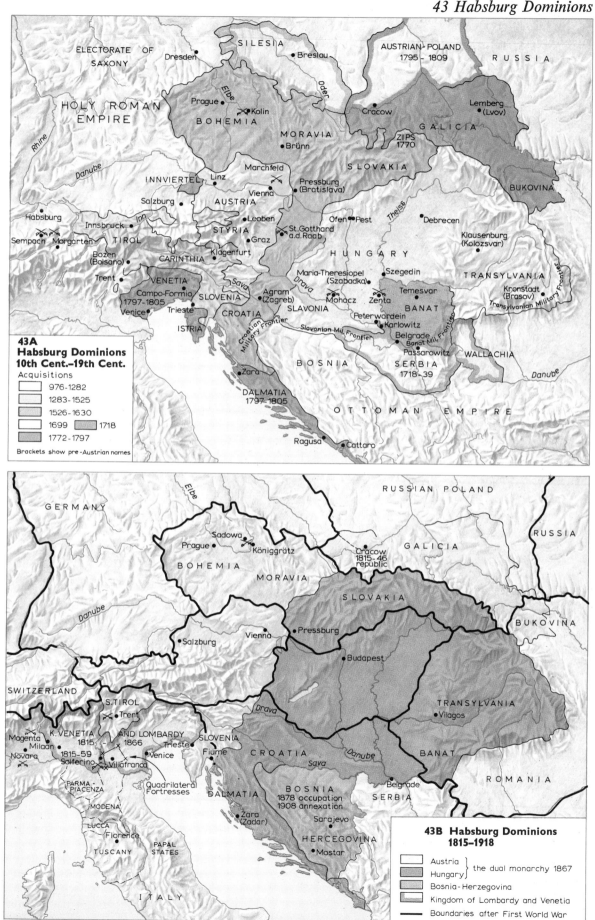

ELECTORATE OF SAXONY

SILESIA

AUSTRIAN-POLAND 1795-1809

RUSSIA

Dresden

Breslau

HOLY ROMAN EMPIRE

Elbe

Prague

Kolin

BOHEMIA

MORAVIA

Brünn

Oder

Cracow

GALICIA

Lemberg (Lvov)

ZIPS 1770

SLOVAKIA

BUKOVINA

Rhine

Danube

INNVIERTEL

Linz

Marchfeld

Pressburg (Bratislava)

Theiss

Salzburg

Vienna

AUSTRIA

Habsburg

Inn

Innsbruck

Leoben

Ofen Pest

Debrecen

Sempach Morgarten

TIROL

STYRIA

St. Gotthard a.d. Raab

Klausenburg (Kolozsvar)

Bozen (Bolsano)

Graz

HUNGARY

Trent

CARINTHIA

Klagenfurt

Maria-Theresiopel (Szabadka)

Szegedin

TRANSYLVANIA

VENETIA

Sava

Kronstadt (Brasov)

Campo-Formio 1797-1805

SLOVENIA

Drava

Mohacz

Zenta

Temesvar

Transylvanian Military Frontier

Venice

Agram (Zagreb)

Trieste

SLAVONIA

BANAT

ISTRIA

CROATIA

Peterwardein

Karlowitz

Croatian Military Frontier

Slavonian Mil. Frontier

Belgrade

Banat Mil. Frontier

Passarowitz

WALLACHIA

43A
Habsburg Dominions
10th Cent.–19th Cent.

Acquisitions

	976-1282
	1283-1525
	1526-1630
	1699 ▨ 1718
	1772-1797

Brackets show pre-Austrian names

BOSNIA

SERBIA 1718-39

Danube

OTTOMAN EMPIRE

Zara

DALMATIA 1797-1805

Ragusa

Cattaro

GERMANY

Elbe

RUSSIAN POLAND

RUSSIA

BOHEMIA

Sadowa

Königgrätz

Prague

MORAVIA

Cracow 1815-46 republic

GALICIA

BUKOVINA

Danube

SLOVAKIA

SWITZERLAND

Salzburg

Vienna

Pressburg

Budapest

S. TIROL

Trent

Drava

TRANSYLVANIA

Magenta

K. VENETIA 1815

AND LOMBARDY 1866

SLOVENIA

Vilagos

Milaan

Trieste

Fiume

Novara

1815-59

Venice

CROATIA

BANAT

Solferino

Villafranca

Sava

Danube

ROMANIA

PARMA - PIACENZA

Quadrilateral Fortresses

DALMATIA

Belgrade

MODENA

BOSNIA

SERBIA

LUCCA

1878 occupation 1908 annexation

Florence

Zara (Zadar)

Sarajevo

PAPAL STATES

TUSCANY

HERCEGOVINA

Mostar

43B Habsburg Dominions
1815-1918

ITALY

	Austria ⎫
	Hungary ⎬ the dual monarchy 1867
	Bosnia-Herzegovina
	Kingdom of Lombardy and Venetia
▬▬	Boundaries after First World War

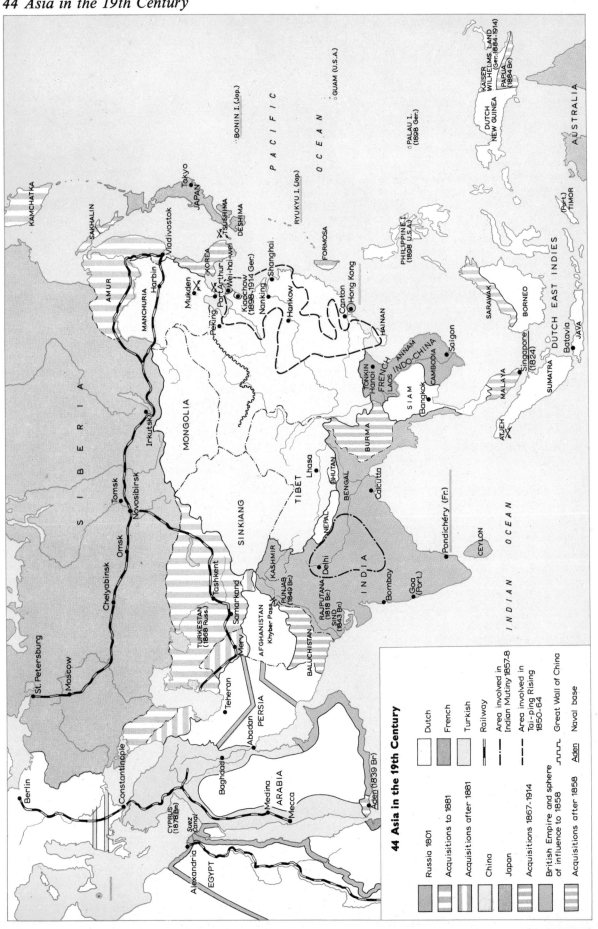

44 Asia in the 19th Century

	Russia 1801		Dutch
	Acquisitions to 1881		French
	Acquisitions after 1881		Turkish
	China		Railway
	Japan		Area involved in Indian Mutiny 1857-8
	Acquisitions 1867-1914		Area involved in Tai-ping Rising 1850-64
	British Empire and sphere of influence to 1858		Great Wall of China
	Acquisitions after 1858	Aden	Naval base

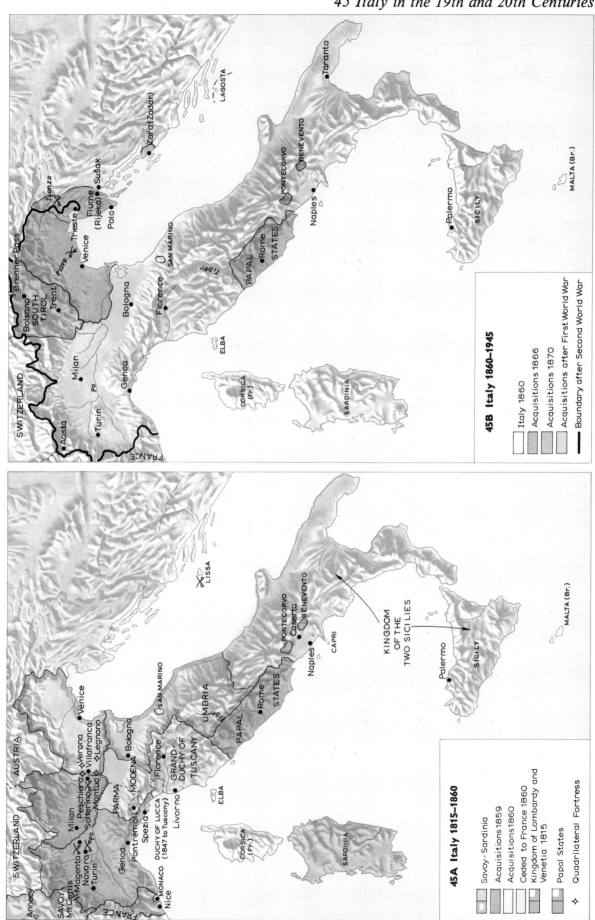

45B Italy 1860–1945

Italy 1860
Acquisitions 1866
Acquisitions 1870
Acquisitions after First World War
Boundary after Second World War

SWITZERLAND
Brenner Pass
Isonzo
Suŝak
Fiume (Rijeka)
Pola
Trieste
Piave
Venice
SOUTH TIROL
Bolsano
Trent
FRANCE
Aosta
Turin
Milan
Po
Genoa
Bologna
Florence
Tiber
SAN MARINO
PAPAL STATES
Rome
PONTECORVO
BENEVENTO
Naples
ELBA
CORSICA (Fr.)
SARDINIA
Palermo
SICILY
Taranto
MALTA (Br.)
Zara (Zadar)
LAGOSTA

45A Italy 1815–1860

Savoy-Sardinia
Acquisitions 1859
Acquisitions 1860
Ceded to France 1860
Kingdom of Lombardy and Venetia 1815
Papal States
Quadrilateral Fortress

SWITZERLAND
AUSTRIA
Annecy
Mt.Cenis
SAVOY
Nice
MONACO
Turin
Novara
Magenta
Milan
Verona
Peschiera
Solferino
Mantua
Legnano
Villafranca
Venice
Po
Genoa
Pontremoli
Spezia
PARMA
MODENA
DUCHY OF LUCCA (1847 to Tuscany)
Livorno
Bologna
Florence
GRAND-DUCHY OF TUSCANY
SAN MARINO
UMBRIA
PAPAL STATES
Tiber
Rome
PONTECORVO
Caserta
BENEVENTO
Naples
CAPRI
KINGDOM OF THE TWO SICILIES
ELBA
CORSICA (Fr.)
SARDINIA
Palermo
SICILY
MALTA (Br.)
LISSA
FRANCE

46 The Unification of Germany

Prussia 1815
Prussia 1866
The North German Federation 1867-71
Germany before the Franco-Prussian War
Alsace-Lorraine
Austria-Hungary 1867
The German Confederation 1815

GREAT BRITAIN

London

DENMARK

Copenhagen

Königsberg

PRUSSIA

Danzig

Vistula

Warsaw

POLAND

RUSSIA

GALICIA

POMERANIA

POSEN

Oder

Breslau

STRELITZ

SILESIA

Dresden

Königgrätz

HUNGARY

Budapest

MECKLENBURG SCHWERIN

BRANDENBURG

Berlin

Leipzig

K. OF SAXONY

Sadowa

Prague

BOHEMIA

AUSTRIA-

Danube

Vienna

STYRIA

CROATIA

Trieste

OTTOMAN EMPIRE

Lübeck

Hamburg

Bremen

Elbe

HOLSTEIN

SCHLESWIG

Düppel

PROV. OF SAXONY

ANHALT

Langensalza

THURINGIAN STATES

CARINTHIA

Venice

HANOVER

OLDENBURG

BRUNSWICK

WESTPHALIA

HESSE-CASSEL

HESSE-DARM-STADT

Frankfurt a. M.

H. D. (southern part)

Munich

BAVARIA

TIROL

Milan

KINGDOM OF THE NETHERLANDS

LIMBURG (member of the German Confederation 1839-66)

KINGDOM OF BELGIUM

RHINE PROVINCE

NASSAU

G. D. LUXEM-BURG

Sedan

Rhine

BAVARIAN PALATINATE

WÜRTTEMBERG

Strasbourg

BADEN

D. HOHENZOLLERN

SWITZERLAND

Metz

ALSACE (Ger. 1871-1919)

LORRAINE

Belfort

Paris

Versailles

(to Belgium 1839)

(left the German Confederation 1866)

FRANCE

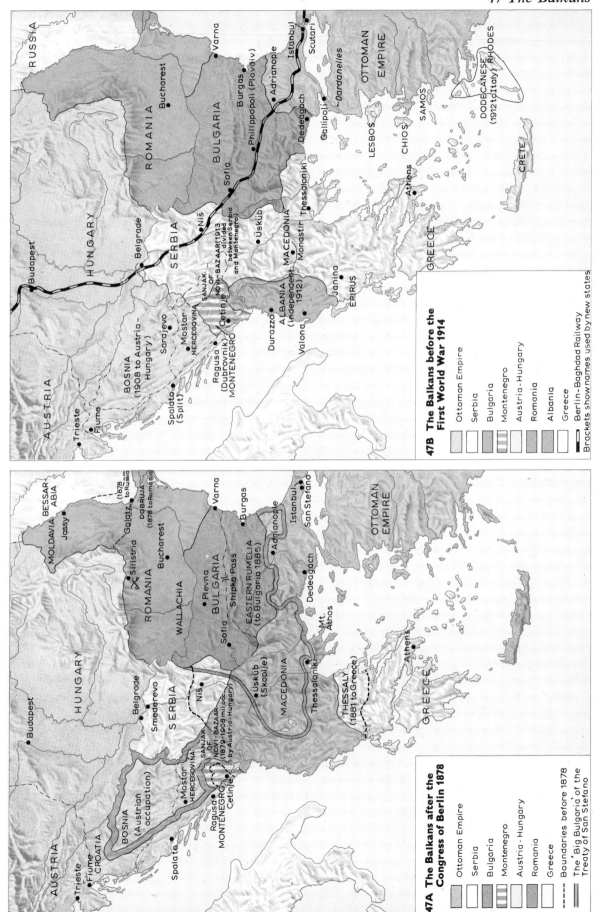

47B The Balkans before the First World War 1914

Ottoman Empire
Serbia
Bulgaria
Montenegro
Austria-Hungary
Romania
Albania
Greece
Berlin-Baghdad Railway
Brackets show names used by new states

RUSSIA
ROMANIA
Bucharest
Varna
Burgas
Philippopoli (Plovdiv)
BULGARIA
Sofia
Istanbul
Adrianople
Dedeagach
Gallipoli
Dardanelles
Scutari
OTTOMAN EMPIRE
DODECANESE (1912 to Italy)
RHODES
HUNGARY
Budapest
Belgrade
SERBIA
Niš
Üsküb
MACEDONIA
Monastir (1912)
Thessaloniki
LESBOS
CHIOS
SAMOS
Athens
GREECE
CRETE
SANJAK OF NOVI-BAZAAR (1913 divided between Serbia and Montenegro)
Cetinje
MONTENEGRO
Ragusa (Dubrovnik)
Mostar
HERCEGOVINA
Sarajevo
BOSNIA (1908 to Austria-Hungary)
Spalato (Split)
Durazzo
Valona
ALBANIA (independent 1912)
Janina
EPIRUS
AUSTRIA
Trieste
Fiume

47A The Balkans after the Congress of Berlin 1878

Ottoman Empire
Serbia
Bulgaria
Montenegro
Austria-Hungary
Romania
Greece
Boundaries before 1878
The 'Big Bulgaria' of the Treaty of San Stefano

BESSARABIA (1878 to Russia)
MOLDAVIA
Jassy
Galatz
DOBRUJA (1878 to Romania)
Silistria
Varna
Burgas
ROMANIA
Bucharest
WALLACHIA
Plevna
BULGARIA
Shipka Pass
Sofia
EASTERN RUMELIA (to Bulgaria 1885)
Adrianople
Istanbul
San Stefano
Dedeagach
Mt. Athos
OTTOMAN EMPIRE
HUNGARY
Budapest
Belgrade
Smederevo
SERBIA
Niš
Üsküb (Skopje)
MACEDONIA
Thessaloniki
THESSALY (1881 to Greece)
Athens
GREECE
SANJAK OF NOVI-BAZAAR (1879-1908 mil.occ by Austria-Hungary)
Cetinje
MONTENEGRO
Ragusa
Mostar
HERCEGOVINA
BOSNIA (Austrian occupation)
Spalato
AUSTRIA
Trieste
Fiume
CROATIA

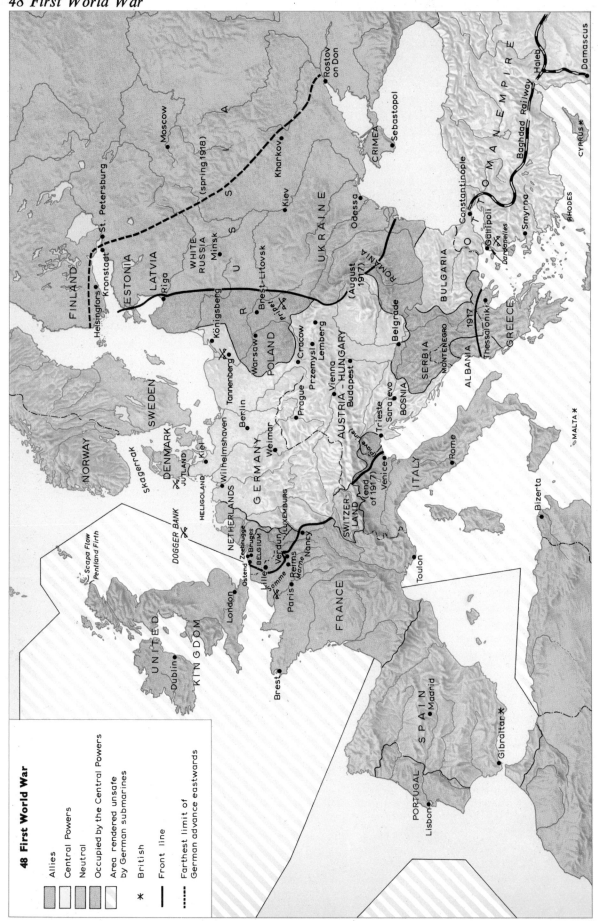

48 First World War

Allies

Central Powers

Neutral

Occupied by the Central Powers

Area rendered unsafe
by German submarines

* British

Front line

Farthest limit of
German advance eastwards

Rostov
on Don

Moscow

(spring 1918)

St. Petersburg

R U S S I A

Kharkov

Kiev

Kronstadt

Helsingfors

FINLAND

ESTONIA

LATVIA

Riga

WHITE
RUSSIA

Minsk

Odessa

UKRAINE

Sebastopol

CRIMEA

Constantinople

O T T O M A N E M P I R E

Haleb

Baghdad Railway

Damascus

CYPRUS *

RHODES

Smyrna

Gallipoli

Dardanelles

(August 1917)

ROMANIA

BULGARIA

Belgrade

GREECE

Thessaloniki

1917

ALBANIA

MONTENEGRO

SERBIA

Sarajevo

BOSNIA

Königsberg

Brest-Litovsk

Pripet

R U S S I A

Warsaw

POLAND

Cracow

Tannenberg

Przemysl

Lemberg

AUSTRIA - HUNGARY

Vienna

Budapest

Prague

Berlin

Weimar

GERMANY

Wilhelmshaven

Kiel

JUTLAND

DENMARK

HELIGOLAND

NETHERLANDS

Bruges

Ostend

Zeebrugge

BELGIUM

LUXEMBURG

Verdun

Reims

Marne

Nancy

Paris

Lille

Somme

FRANCE

Brest

Trieste

Isonzo line

Venice

(end of 1917)

SWITZER-
LAND

ITALY

Rome

Bizerta

Toulon

MALTA *

SWEDEN

NORWAY

Skagerrak

DOGGER BANK

Scapa Flow

Pentland Firth

UNITED

KINGDOM

Dublin

London

PORTUGAL

Lisbon

S P A I N

Madrid

Gibraltar *

49 Soviet Russia 1917–48

Russia to 1917

Soviet Russia 1917-39·

Acquired from Germany
and Czechoslovakia 1945

Satellite states
(after 1948)

Countries in Western
alliances after 1945

Boundary of Russia
after Second World War

NORWAY

S W E D E N

F I N L A N D

Petsamo
(Pechenga)

Murmansk

K O L A

Pustozersk

Archangel

ALAND I.

Helsinki

Lake
Ladoga

Hangö

BALTIC
SEA

Reval

Kronstadt

Petrograd
(Leningrad)

U N I O N   O F

ESTONIA

LATVIA

Riga

Perm

Daugavpils

Kalinin

S O V I E T   S O C I A L I S T

Moscow

Gorki

Kazan

GER-
MANY

Kaunas

LITHUANIA

Vitebsk

Smolensk

Vilna

Kaluga

Tula

Samara
(Kuibyshev)

Warsaw

Grodno

Minsk

WHITE RUSSIA

R E P U B L I C S

Brest-Litovsk

Orel

Volga

Saratov

POLAND

Voronezh

Cracow

Lemberg

Kiev

CZECHO-
SLOVAKIA

Dnieper

Stalingrad
(Volgograd)

CALMUCKS

TRANS-
CARPATHIA

U K R A I N E

Astrakhan

MOLDAVIA

DON COSSACKS

ROMANIA

Odessa

Kherson

Rostow

Bucharest

CRIMEA

Danube

Sebastopol

Tuapse

C A S P I A N

BULGARIA

B L A C K   S E A

SEA

GREECE

Contantinople

Bosphorus

Batumi

GEORGIA

Tiflis

Dardanelles

T   U   R   K   E   Y

Kars

Baku

Ankara

TRANSCAUCASIA

PERSIA (IRAN)

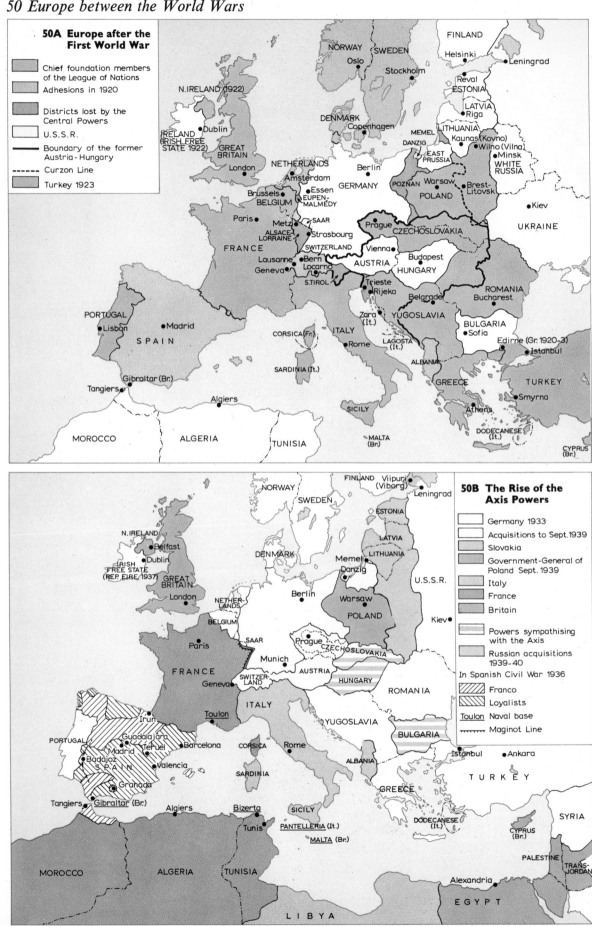

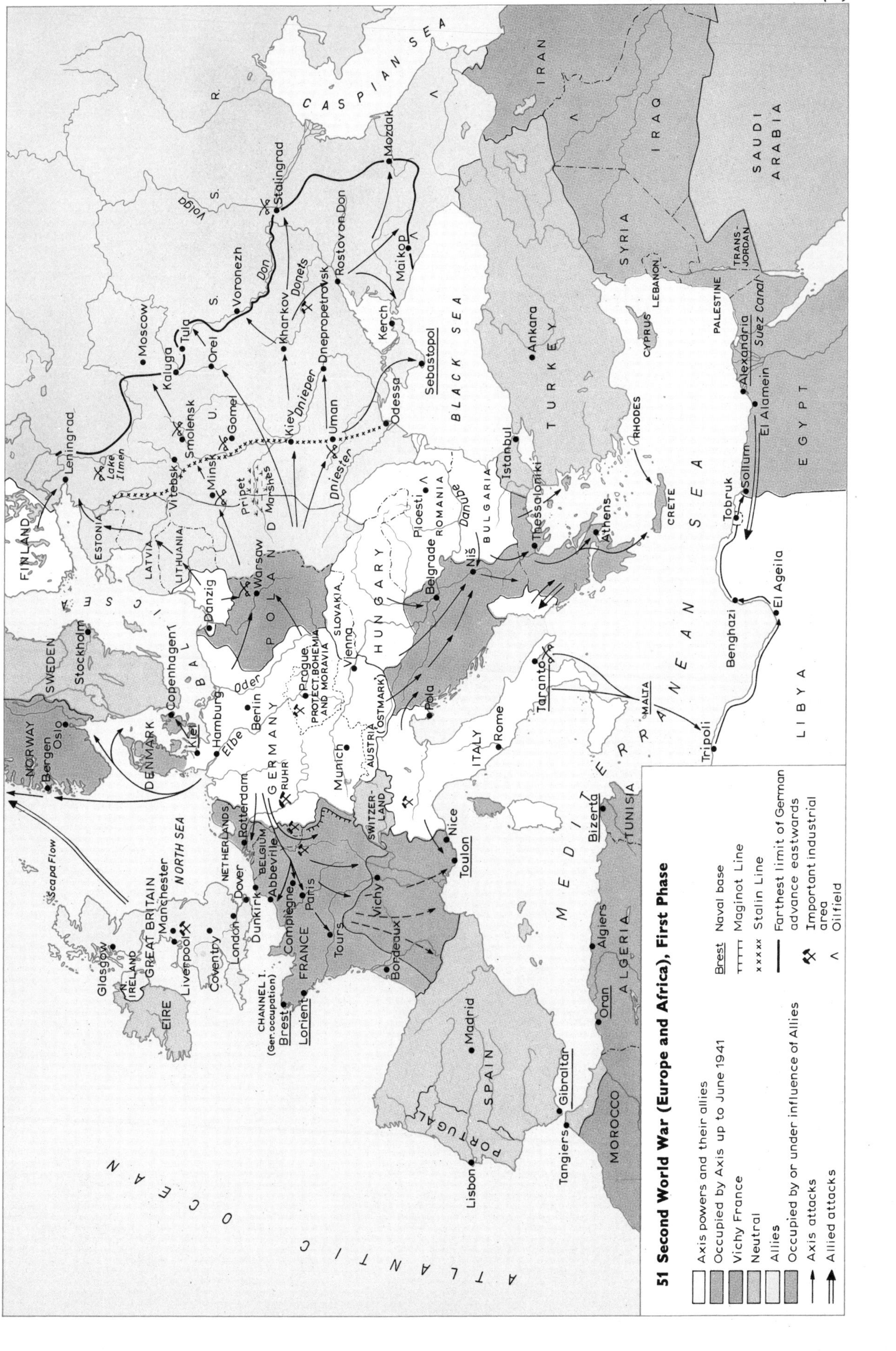

51 Second World War (Europe and Africa), First Phase

Legend:

- Axis powers and their allies
- Occupied by Axis up to June 1941
- Vichy France
- Neutral
- Allies
- Occupied by or under influence of Allies
- → Axis attacks
- ⇒ Allied attacks

- Brest — Naval base
- ┬┬┬┬ Maginot Line
- xxxxx Stalin Line
- —— Farthest limit of German advance eastwards
- ✗ Important industrial area
- ∧ Oilfield

Place names and labels:

CASPIAN SEA · IRAN · IRAQ · SAUDI ARABIA · SYRIA · TRANS-JORDAN · LEBANON · PALESTINE · CYPRUS · TURKEY · Ankara · Istanbul · Suez Canal · Alexandria · El Alamein · EGYPT · Sollum · Tobruk · El Agheila · Benghazi · LIBYA · Tripoli

Mozdok · Stalingrad · Maikop · Rostov-on-Don · Dnepropetrovsk · Kharkov · Donets · Voronezh · Don · Volga · R. S. · U. S. S. R. · Moscow · Tula · Kaluga · Orel · Kiev · Dnieper · Uman · Odessa · Kerch · Sebastopol · BLACK SEA · Smolensk · Gomel · Mins · Vitebsk · Pripet · P. MARSHES · Dniester · Leningrad · Lake Ilmen · FINLAND · ESTONIA · LATVIA · LITHUANIA · Danzig · Warsaw · POLAND · Oder

Thessaloniki · Athens · CRETE · RHODES · MALTA · Niš · Belgrade · Ploesti · ROMANIA · BULGARIA · Danube · HUNGARY · Vienna · SLOVAKIA · AUSTRIA (OSTMARK) · Pola · Taranto · Rome · ITALY · Bizerta · TUNISIA · MEDITERRANEAN SEA

PROTECT. BOHEMIA AND MORAVIA · Prague · GERMANY · Berlin · Elbe · Hamburg · Kiel · Munich · RUHR · SWITZERLAND · Nice · Toulon · Vichy · FRANCE · Paris · Compiègne · Tours · Bordeaux · Abbeville · BELGIUM · NETHERLANDS · Rotterdam · Dunkirk · Dover · London · Coventry · Brest · Lorient · CHANNEL I. (Ger. occupation)

SWEDEN · Stockholm · NORWAY · Oslo · Bergen · DENMARK · Copenhagen · BALTIC SEA · NORTH SEA · Scapa Flow · GREAT BRITAIN · Glasgow · Manchester · Liverpool · N. IRELAND · EIRE · ATLANTIC OCEAN

SPAIN · Madrid · PORTUGAL · Lisbon · Tangiers · Gibraltar · MOROCCO · ALGERIA · Oran · Algiers

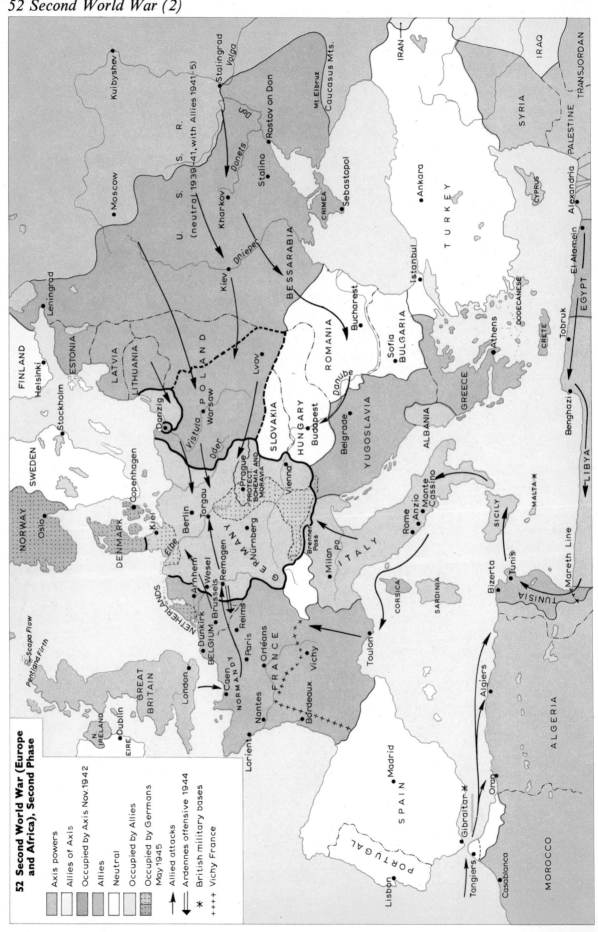

52 Second World War (Europe and Africa), Second Phase

Axis powers
Allies of Axis
Occupied by Axis Nov.1942
Allies
Neutral
Occupied by Allies
Occupied by Germans May 1945
Allied attacks
Ardennes offensive 1944
British military bases
Vichy France

53 Second World War (the Pacific)

Japanese Empire 1919	→ Japanese offensives
Conquered to Dec. 1941	⌐⌐⌐⌐⌐➤ Japanese air raids
Conquered to April 1942	→ Allied offensives
☆ U.S.A. (and bases)	➤ Allied air raids
✳ Br. Commonwealth (and bases)	*JAVA SEA 27-2-42* Japanese victory
China	OKINAWA 1-4-45 Allied victory
Soviet Russia and Mongolia	▫ Atom bomb attack
	⊤⊤⊤⊤⊤⊤ Burma Road

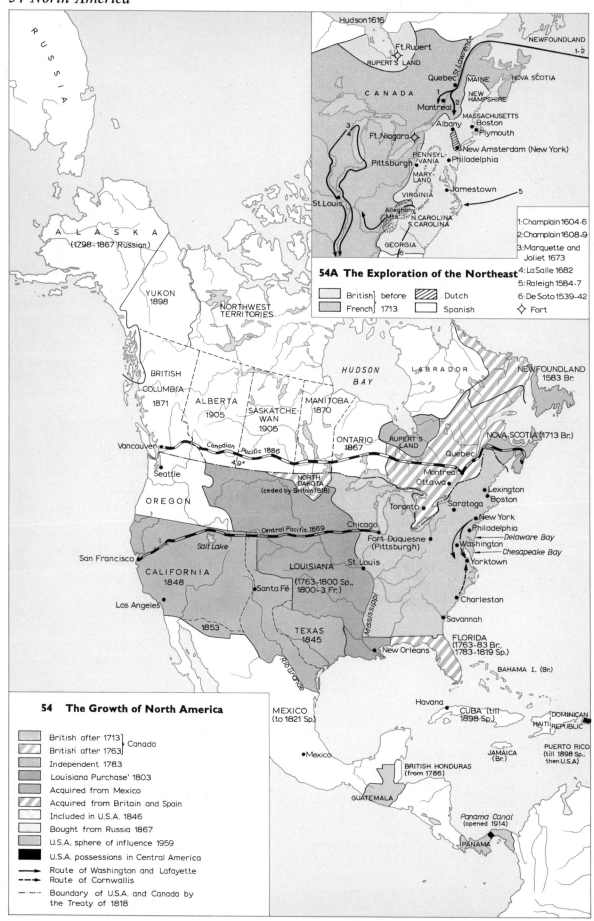

54A The Exploration of the Northeast

| British | before | Dutch |
| French | 1713 | Spanish |

Fort ◇

1: Champlain 1604-6
2: Champlain 1608-9
3: Marquette and Joliet 1673
4: La Salle 1682
5: Raleigh 1584-7
6: De Soto 1539-42

54   The Growth of North America

- British after 1713 } Canada
- British after 1763 }
- Independent 1783
- Louisiana Purchase' 1803
- Acquired from Mexico
- Acquired from Britain and Spain
- Included in U.S.A. 1846
- Bought from Russia 1867
- U.S.A. sphere of influence 1959
- U.S.A. possessions in Central America
- → Route of Washington and Lafayette
- --→ Route of Cornwallis
- ·—·— Boundary of U.S.A. and Canada by the Treaty of 1818

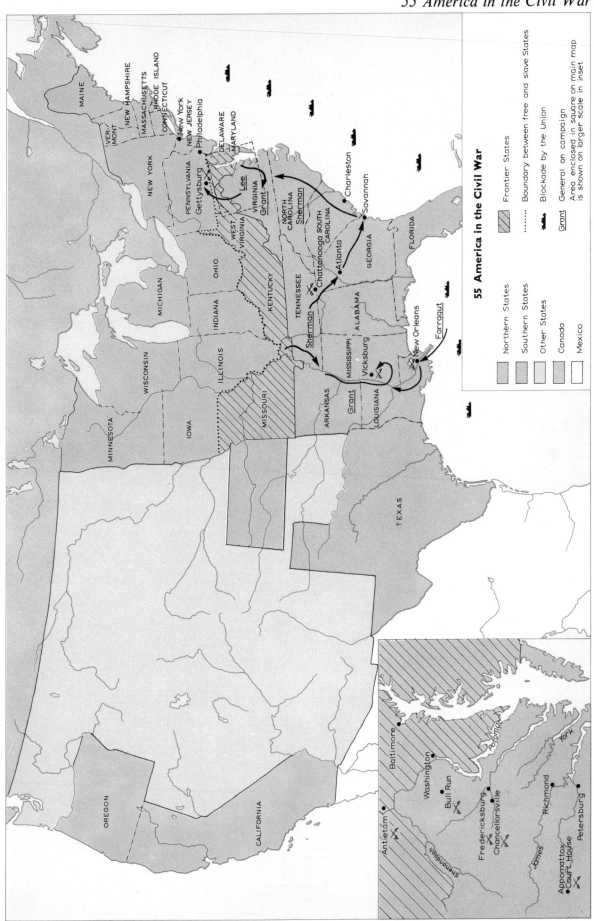

55 America in the Civil War

Northern States

Southern States

Other States

Canada

Mexico

Frontier States

Boundary between free and slave States

Blockade by the Union

General on campaign

Grant

Area enclosed in square on main map is shown on larger scale in inset

MAINE

NEW HAMPSHIRE

VERMONT

MASSACHUSETTS

RHODE ISLAND

CONNECTICUT

New York

NEW JERSEY

Philadelphia

DELAWARE

MARYLAND

NEW YORK

PENNSYLVANIA

Gettysburg

Lee

Grant

VIRGINIA

WEST VIRGINIA

NORTH CAROLINA

Charleston

Savannah

Sherman

SOUTH CAROLINA

OHIO

KENTUCKY

TENNESSEE

Chattanooga

Atlanta

GEORGIA

FLORIDA

MICHIGAN

INDIANA

ILLINOIS

WISCONSIN

MINNESOTA

IOWA

MISSOURI

ARKANSAS

Sherman

ALABAMA

MISSISSIPPI

Vicksburg

LOUISIANA

Grant

New Orleans

Farragut

TEXAS

OREGON

CALIFORNIA

Baltimore

Washington

Bull Run

Antietam

Fredericksburg

Chancellorsville

Shenandoah

Potomac

Rappahannock

York

James

Richmond

Petersburg

Appomattox Court House

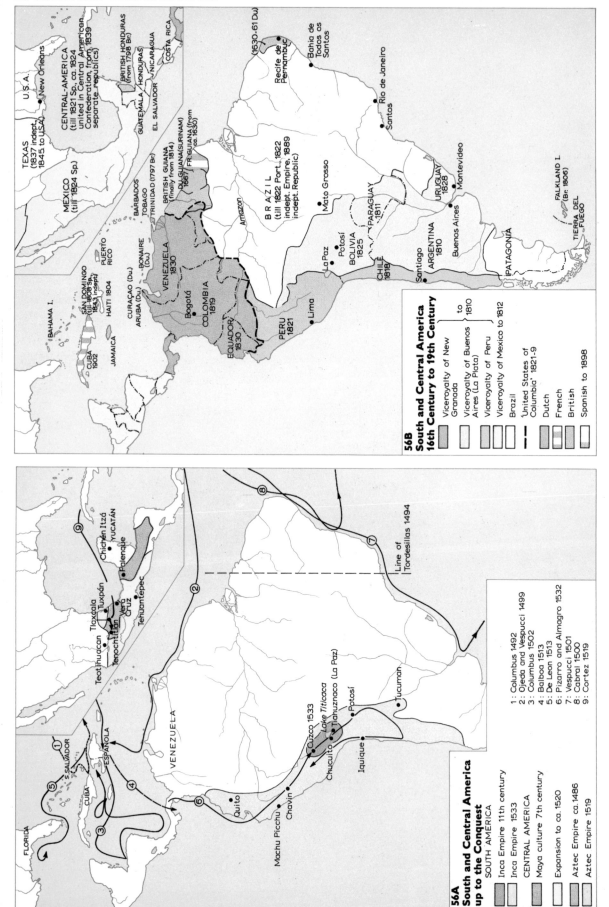

56B
South and Central America
16th Century to 19th Century

Viceroyalty of New Granada
Viceroyalty of Buenos Aires (La Plata) } to 1810
Viceroyalty of Peru
Viceroyalty of Mexico to 1812

Brazil

'United States of Columbia' 1821-9

Dutch
French
British
Spanish to 1898

(1630-61 Du.)
Recife de Pernambuc
Bahia de Todos os Santos
Rio de Janeiro
Santos
Montevideo
URUGUAY 1828
FALKLAND I. (Br. 1806)
TIERRA DEL FUEGO
PATAGONIA
Buenos Aires
ARGENTINA 1810
Santiago
CHILE 1818
BOLIVIA 1825
Potosí
PARAGUAY 1811
Mato Grosso
La Paz
B R A Z I L (till 1822 Port., 1822 indept. Empire, 1889 indept. Republic)
Amazon
Lima
PERU 1821
EQUADOR 1830
COLOMBIA 1819
Bogotá
VENEZUELA 1830
DU GUIANA/SURINAM 1667 (from ca. 1630)
FR. GUIANA (from 1814)
BRITISH GUIANA (finally from 1814)
TRINIDAD (1797 Br.)
TOBAGO
BARBADOS
BONAIRE (Du.)
ARUBA (Du.)
CURAÇAO (Du.)
PUERTO RICO
HAITI 1804
SAN DOMINGO (till 1808 Sp., 1843 indept.)
CUBA 1902
JAMAICA
BAHAMA I.
NICARAGUA
COSTA RICA
EL SALVADOR
HONDURAS
GUATEMALA
BRITISH HONDURAS (from 1798 Br.)
CENTRAL-AMERICA (till 1821 Sp., ca. 1824 united in Central American Confederation, from 1839 separate republics)
MEXICO (till 1824 Sp.)
New Orleans
U.S.A.
TEXAS (1837 indept., 1845 to USA)

56A
South and Central America
up to the Conquest
SOUTH AMERICA

Inca Empire 11th century
Inca Empire 1533
CENTRAL AMERICA
Maya culture 7th century
Expansion to ca. 1520
Aztec Empire ca. 1486
Aztec Empire 1519

1: Columbus 1492
2: Ojeda and Vespucci 1499
3: Columbus 1502
4: Balboa 1513
5: De Leon 1513
6: Pizarro and Almagro 1532
7: Vespucci 1501
8: Cabral 1500
9: Cortez 1519

Line of Tordesillas 1494

FLORIDA
S. SALVADOR
CUBA
ESPAÑOLA
YUCATÁN
Chichén Itzá
Palenque
Tuxpán
Tlaxcala
Teotihuacan
Tenochtitlan
Vera Cruz
Tehuantepec
VENEZUELA
Quito
Chavin
Machu Picchu
Iquique
Chucuito
Cuzco 1533
Lake Titicaca
Tiahuznaco (La Paz)
Potosí
Tucuman

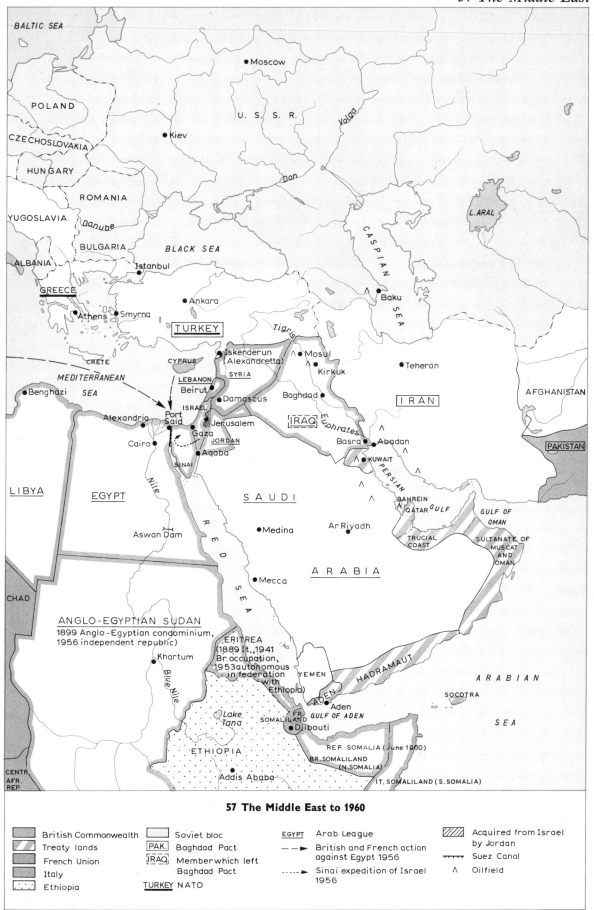

BALTIC SEA

POLAND

CZECHOSLOVAKIA

HUNGARY

ROMANIA

YUGOSLAVIA · Danube

BULGARIA

ALBANIA

GREECE

•Moscow

U. S. S. R.

•Kiev

Volga

Don

BLACK SEA

•Istanbul

L. ARAL

CASPIAN SEA

•Baku

•Ankara

TURKEY

CRETE

MEDITERRANEAN

SEA

Tigris

Iskenderun
(Alexandretta)

CYPRUS

LEBANON

SYRIA

•Mosul

•Kirkuk

•Teheran

AFGHANISTAN

•Benghazi

Beirut

•Damascus

ISRAEL

Baghdad

IRAN

Euphrates

IRAQ

PAKISTAN

•Athens ·Smyrna

•Alexandria

Port
Said

Cairo

•Jerusalem

Gaza

JORDAN

•Aqaba

SINAI

Basra

•Abadan

•KUWAIT

PERSIAN

LIBYA

EGYPT

Nile

SAUDI

•Medina

Ar Riyadh

BAHREIN
QATAR

GULF

GULF OF
OMAN

TRUCIAL
COAST

SULTANATE OF
MUSCAT
AND
OMAN

Aswan Dam

RED

SEA

ARABIA

•Mecca

CHAD

ANGLO-EGYPTIAN SUDAN
1899 Anglo-Egyptian condominium,
1956 independent republic)

•Khartum

Blue Nile

ERITREA
(1889 It.,1941
Br.occupation,
1953 autonomous
in federation
with
Ethiopia)

YEMEN

HADRAMAUT

ARABIAN

SOCOTRA

SEA

Lake
Tana

FR.
SOMALILAND

ADEN

•Aden

GULF OF ADEN

•Djibouti

CENTR.
AFR.
REP

ETHIOPIA

•Addis Ababa

REP. SOMALIA (June 1960)

BR.SOMALILAND
(N.SOMALIA)

IT. SOMALILAND (S.SOMALIA)

57 The Middle East to 1960

British Commonwealth	Soviet bloc	EGYPT Arab League	Acquired from Israel by Jordan
Treaty lands	PAK. Baghdad Pact	– –▶ British and French action against Egypt 1956	Suez Canal
French Union	IRAQ Member which left	····▶ Sinai expedition of Israel 1956	∧ Oilfield
Italy	Baghdad Pact		
Ethiopia	TURKEY NATO		

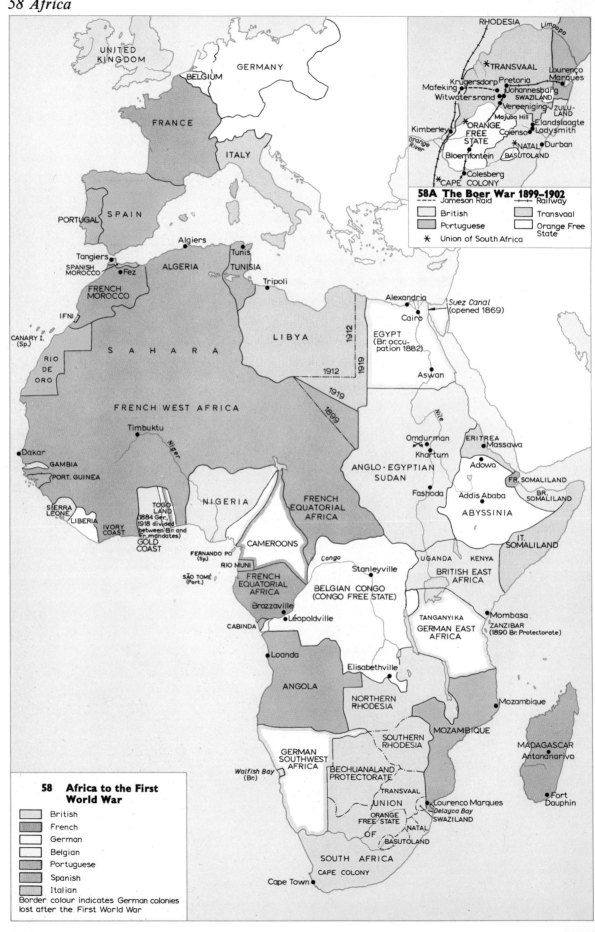

UNITED KINGDOM

GERMANY

BELGIUM

FRANCE

ITALY

PORTUGAL

SPAIN

RHODESIA

Limpopo

★ TRANSVAAL
Krugersdorp Pretoria Lourenço
Mafeking Johannesburg Marques
Witwatersrand SWAZILAND
Vereeniging ZULU-
Majuba Hill LAND
Kimberley ★ORANGE Elandslaagte
FREE Colenso Ladysmith
Orange River STATE ★NATAL Durban
Bloemfontein BASUTOLAND
Colesberg
★CAPE COLONY

58A The Boer War 1899–1902
- - - Jameson Raid   +—+— Railway
☐ British   ☐ Transvaal
☐ Portuguese   ☐ Orange Free State
★ Union of South Africa

Algiers
Tangiers Tunis
SPANISH ALGERIA TUNISIA
MOROCCO Fez
FRENCH Tripoli
MOROCCO
IFNI
CANARY I.
(Sp.)
RIO S A H A R A LIBYA EGYPT
DE (Br. occu-
ORO pation 1882)

Alexandria Suez Canal
Cairo (opened 1869)

Aswan

1912

1912

1919

1899

FRENCH WEST AFRICA

Timbuktu

Niger

Nile

Dakar
GAMBIA
PORT. GUINEA
SIERRA
LEONE
LIBERIA
IVORY
COAST
GOLD
COAST

TOGO-
LAND
1884 Ger.,
1918 divided
between Br.
and Fr.
mandates)

NIGERIA

FERNANDO PO
(Sp.)
RIO MUNI
SÃO TOMÉ
(Port.)

CAMEROONS

FRENCH
EQUATORIAL
AFRICA

FRENCH
EQUATORIAL
AFRICA
Brazzaville
Léopoldville
CABINDA

Congo
Stanleyville

BELGIAN CONGO
(CONGO FREE STATE)

Omdurman
Khartum

ANGLO-EGYPTIAN
SUDAN

Fashoda

ERITREA
Massawa

Adowa

Addis Ababa
ABYSSINIA

FR. SOMALILAND
BR.
SOMALILAND

IT.
SOMALILAND

UGANDA KENYA

BRITISH EAST
AFRICA

Mombasa
ZANZIBAR
(1890 Br. Protectorate)

Loanda

ANGOLA

Elisabethville

NORTHERN
RHODESIA

TANGANYIKA

GERMAN EAST
AFRICA

Mozambique

MADAGASCAR
Antananarivo

SOUTHERN
RHODESIA

MOZAMBIQUE

GERMAN
SOUTHWEST
AFRICA

Walfish Bay
(Br.)

BECHUANALAND
PROTECTORATE

TRANSVAAL

UNION
OF
ORANGE
FREE STATE

SOUTH AFRICA

CAPE COLONY

Cape Town

Lourenço Marques
Delagoa Bay
SWAZILAND
NATAL
BASUTOLAND

Fort
Dauphin

58   Africa to the First World War
☐ British
☐ French
☐ German
☐ Belgian
☐ Portuguese
☐ Spanish
☐ Italian
Border colour indicates German colonies
lost after the First World War

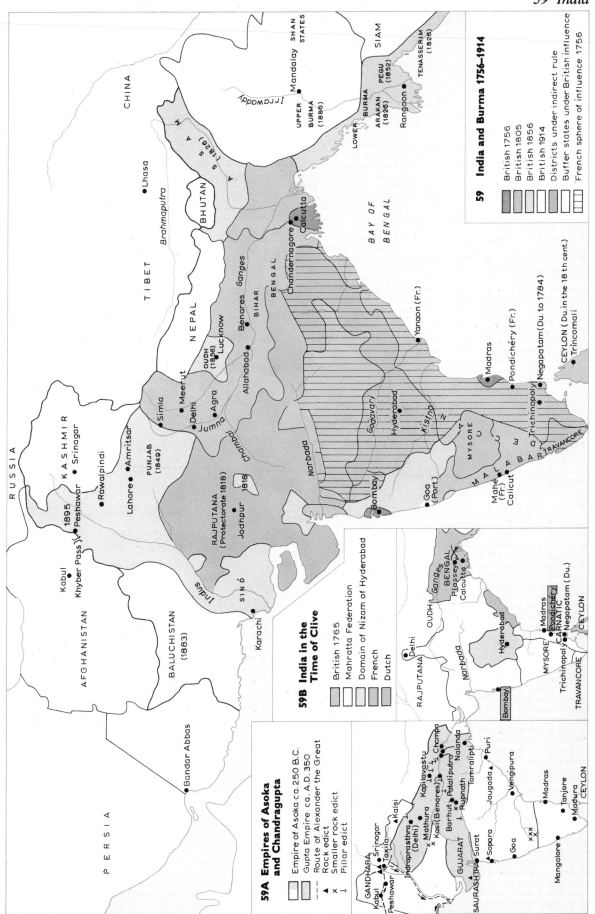

59 India and Burma 1756-1914

- British 1756
- British 1805
- British 1856
- British 1914
- Districts under indirect rule
- Buffer states under British influence
- French sphere of influence 1756

CHINA

SHAN STATES

Mandalay

UPPER BURMA (1886)

Irrawaddy

SIAM

BURMA

LOWER

PEGU (1852)

TENASSERIM (1826)

ARAKAN (1826)

Rangoon

RUSSIA

Lhasa

Brahmaputra

TIBET

BHUTAN

NEPAL

KASHMIR

Srinagar

Rawalpindi

1895 Peshawar

Khyber Pass

Kabul

AFGHANISTAN

Lahore

Amritsar

PUNJAB (1849)

Simla

Meerut

Delhi

Agra

Jumna

Chambal

Lucknow

OUDH (1856)

Benares

Ganges

BIHAR

Allahabad

BENGAL

Calcutta

Chandernagore

BAY OF BENGAL

RAJPUTANA (Protectorate 1818)

Jodhpur

1818

Narbada

Bombay

Godavari

Hyderabad

Kistna

Yanaon (Fr.)

Madras

Pondichéry (Fr.)

Negapatam (Du. to 1784)

CEYLON (Du. in the 18th cent.)

Trincomali

MYSORE

Goa (Port.)

Mahé (Fr.)

Calicut

MALABAR

TRAVANCORE

Trichinopoly

BALUCHISTAN (1883)

SIND

Karachi

Indus

Bandar Abbas

PERSIA

59B India in the Time of Clive

- British 1765
- Mahratta Federation
- Domain of Nizam of Hyderabad
- French
- Dutch

RAJPUTANA

Delhi

OUDH

Ganges

BENGAL

Plassey

Calcutta

Narbada

MYSORE

Hyderabad

Madras

Pondichéry

CARNATIC

Trichinopoly

Negapatam (Du.)

TRAVANCORE

Bombay

CEYLON

59A Empires of Asoka and Chandragupta

- Empire of Asoka ca. 250 B.C.
- Gupta Empire ca. A.D. 350
- ---- Route of Alexander the Great
- ▲ Rock edict
- × Smaller rock edict
- ⊥ Pillar edict

GANDHARA

Kabul

Srinagar

Peshawar

Taxila

Indraprasthna (Delhi)

Mathura

Kalsi

Kapilavastu

Kasi (Benares)

Barhut

Rupnath

SAURASHTRA

GUJARAT

Surat

Sopara

Goa

Mangalore

Champa

Nalanda

Pataliputra

Tamralipti

Puri

Jaugada

Vengipura

Madras

Tanjore

Madura

CEYLON

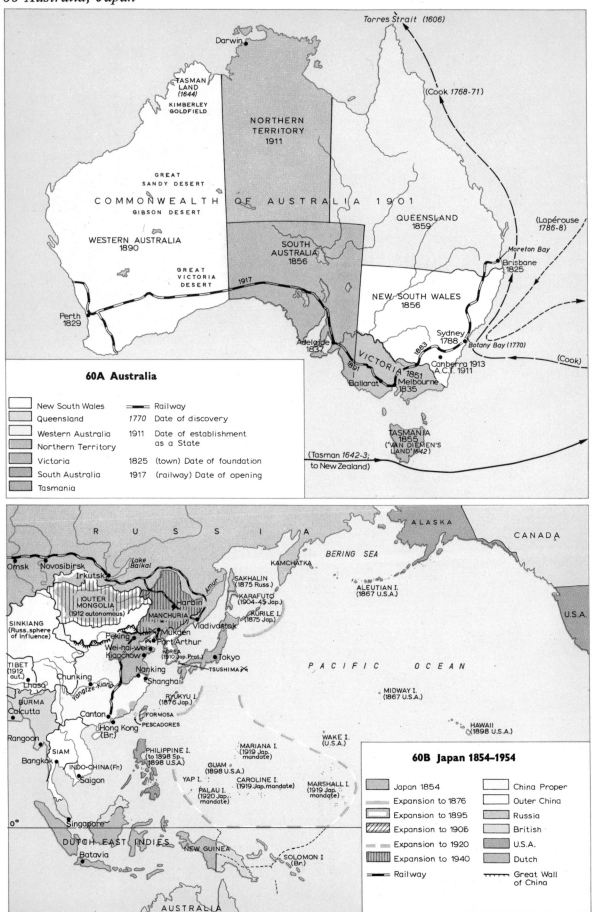

60A Australia

	New South Wales	━━ Railway	
	Queensland	*1770*	Date of discovery
	Western Australia	1911	Date of establishment as a State
	Northern Territory		
	Victoria	1825	(town) Date of foundation
	South Australia	1917	(railway) Date of opening
	Tasmania		

60B Japan 1854–1954

	Japan 1854		China Proper
	Expansion to 1876		Outer China
	Expansion to 1895		Russia
	Expansion to 1905		British
	Expansion to 1920		U.S.A.
	Expansion to 1940		Dutch
	━━ Railway	┅┅┅	Great Wall of China

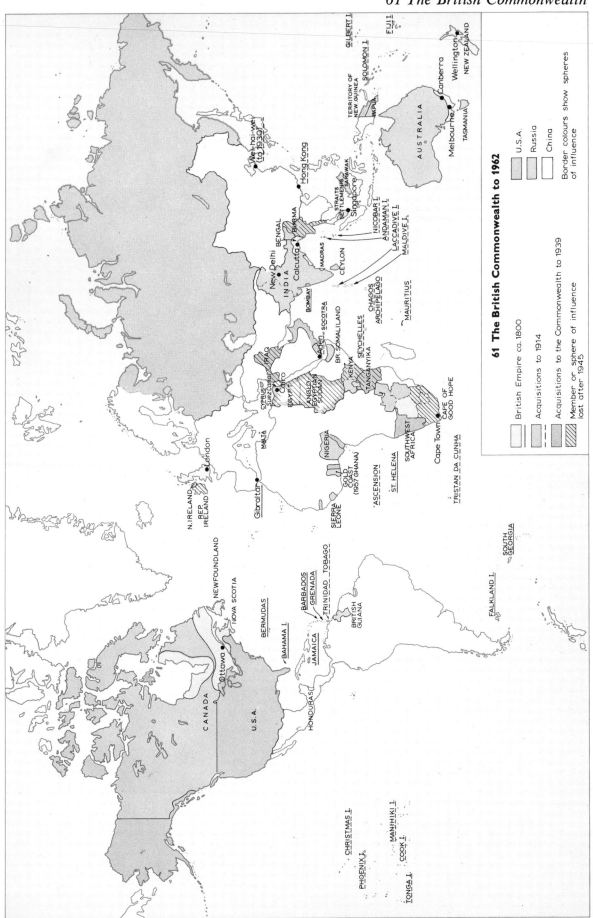

61 The British Commonwealth to 1962

U.S.A.

Russia

China

Border colours show spheres of influence

British Empire ca.1800

Acquisitions to 1914

Acquisitions to the Commonwealth to 1939

Member or sphere of influence lost after 1945

GILBERT I.

FIJI

SOLOMON I.

Wellington
NEW ZEALAND

Canberra
Melbourne
AUSTRALIA
TASMANIA

TERRITORY OF NEW GUINEA
PAPUA

Wei-hai-wei (to 1930)

Hong Kong

BURMA
BENGAL
New Delhi
Calcutta
INDIA
MADRAS
BOMBAY
CEYLON

SARAWAK
STRAITS SETTLEMENTS
Singapore
NICOBAR I.
ANDAMAN I.
LACCADIVE I.
MALDIVE I.

CHAGOS ARCHIPELAGO

MAURITIUS

SOCOTRA
IRAQ
Aden
BR. SOMALILAND
SEYCHELLES
KENYA
TANGANYIKA

CYPRUS
Suez Canal
Cairo
EGYPT
ANGLO-EGYPTIAN SUDAN

MALTA

Gibraltar

N. IRELAND
REP. IRELAND

London

NIGERIA
SIERRA LEONE
GOLD COAST (1957 GHANA)

ASCENSION
ST. HELENA

SOUTHWEST AFRICA
CAPE OF GOOD HOPE
Cape Town

TRISTAN DA CUNHA

SOUTH GEORGIA

FALKLAND I.

NEWFOUNDLAND
NOVA SCOTIA
BERMUDAS
BAHAMA I.
Ottawa
CANADA
U.S.A.
HONDURAS
JAMAICA
BARBADOS
GRENADA
TRINIDAD TOBAGO
BRITISH GUIANA

CHRISTMAS I.
PHOENIX I.
MANIHIKI I.
COOK I.
TONGA I.

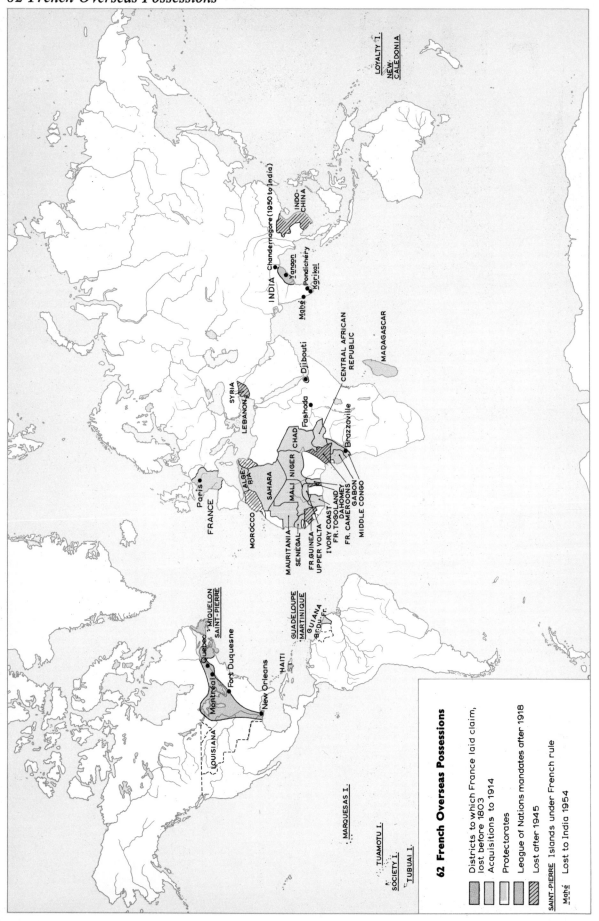

LOYALTY I.

NEW CALEDONIA

Chandernagore (1950 to India)

INDO-CHINA

Yanon

INDIA   Pondichéry
         Karikal

Mahé

Djibouti

CENTRAL AFRICAN
REPUBLIC

MADAGASCAR

SYRIA
LEBANON

Fashoda

Brazzaville

CHAD

Paris

NIGER

ALGERIA

SAHARA   MALI

FRANCE

MOROCCO

MAURITANIA

SENEGAL   FR. TOGOLAND
FR. GUINEA   FR. DAHOMEY
UPPER VOLTA   FR. CAMEROONS
IVORY COAST   GABON
              MIDDLE CONGO

MIQUELON
SAINT-PIERRE

Quebec

GUADELOUPE
MARTINIQUE

Montréal   GUIANA
           FR. DU.

Fort Duquesne

HAITI

New Orleans

LOUISIANA

MARQUESAS I.

TUAMOTU I.

SOCIETY I.

TUBUAI I.

62 French Overseas Possessions

Districts to which France laid claim,
lost before 1803

Acquisitions to 1914

Protectorates

League of Nations mandates after 1918

Lost after 1945

SAINT-PIERRE Islands under French rule

Mahé   Lost to India 1954

63A Central Europe after the Second World War

Russia
Poland and Polish-administered Germany
Russian satellite states
German Democratic Republic
Federal Republic of Germany
Western NATO countries
Neutral
East boundary of Germany 1919
Boundary of East and West Ger.
Boundary of zones
Oder-Neisse Line
Brackets show former German names

63B Europe after the Second World War

Soviet bloc
Yugoslavia
Lost by Poland to Russia 1945
NATO Countries
Lost by Nato
Into Soviet bloc 1948
Iron Curtain

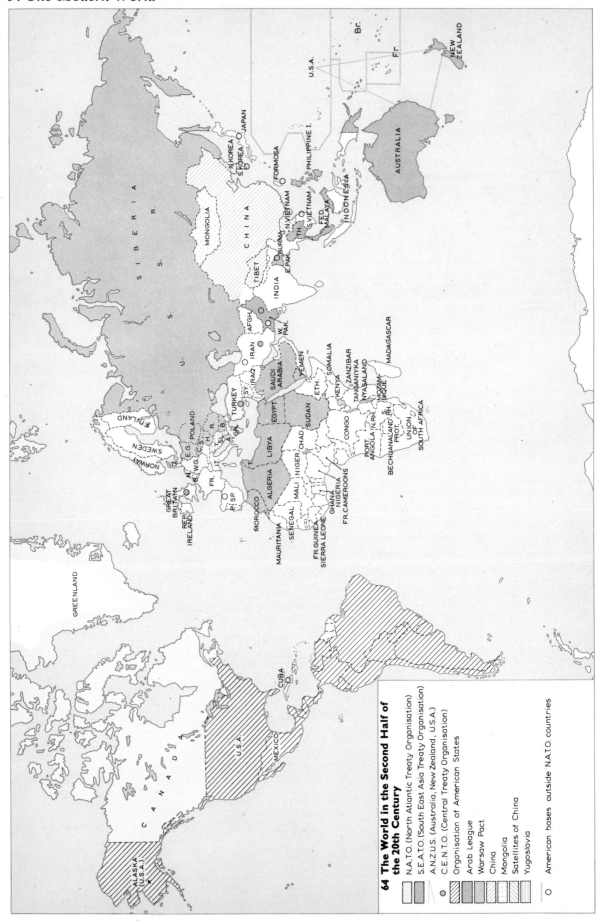

64 The World in the Second Half of the 20th Century

N.A.T.O. (North Atlantic Treaty Organisation)
S.E.A.T.O. (South East Asia Treaty Organisation)
A.N.Z.U.S. (Australia, New Zealand, U.S.A.)
C.E.N.T.O. (Central Treaty Organisation)
Organisation of American States

Arab League
Warsaw Pact
China
Mongolia
Satellites of China
Yugoslavia

American bases outside N.A.T.O. countries

BLACK AND WHITE
SKETCH MAPS

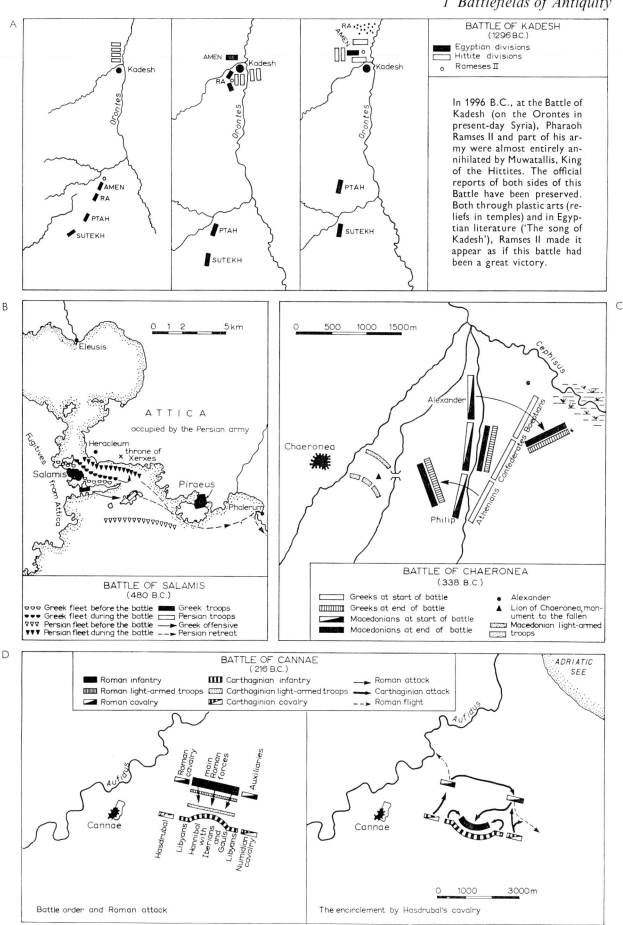

A

BATTLE OF KADESH
(1296 B.C.)

▮ Egyptian divisions
▯ Hittite divisions
○ Rameses II

In 1996 B.C., at the Battle of Kadesh (on the Orontes in present-day Syria), Pharaoh Ramses II and part of his army were almost entirely annihilated by Muwatallis, King of the Hittites. The official reports of both sides of this Battle have been preserved. Both through plastic arts (reliefs in temples) and in Egyptian literature ('The song of Kadesh'), Ramses II made it appear as if this battle had been a great victory.

B

ATTICA

occupied by the Persian army

Eleusis

Heracleum
throne of Xerxes ×

Salamis

Piraeus

Phalerum

Fugitives from Attica

BATTLE OF SALAMIS
(480 B.C.)

ᴗᴗᴗ Greek fleet before the battle   ▮ Greek troops
▼▼▼ Greek fleet during the battle   ▯ Persian troops
▽▽▽ Persian fleet before the battle   → Greek offensive
▼▼▼ Persian fleet during the battle   ⇢ Persian retreat

C

Cephisus

Alexander

Chaeronea

Athenians   Confederates   Boeotians

Philip

BATTLE OF CHAERONEA
(338 B.C.)

▯ Greeks at start of battle   ● Alexander
▥ Greeks at end of battle   ▲ Lion of Chaeronea, monument to the fallen
◪ Macedonians at start of battle   ▦ Macedonian light-armed
▰ Macedonians at end of battle   ▨ troops

D

BATTLE OF CANNAE
(216 B.C.)

▮ Roman infantry   ▥ Carthaginian infantry   → Roman attack
▥ Roman light-armed troops   ▨ Carthaginian light-armed troops   ⟶ Carthaginian attack
▰ Roman cavalry   ◩ Carthaginian cavalry   ⇢ Roman flight

ADRIATIC SEE

Aufidus

Cannae

Roman cavalry
main Roman forces
Auxiliaries
Hasdrubal
Libyans
Hannibal with Iberians and Gauls
Libyans
Numidian cavalry

Battle order and Roman attack

Aufidus

Cannae

0   1000   3000m

The encirclement by Hasdrubal's cavalry

A

BOSPORUS

Turkish fleet 1453

(Pera)
Galata

chain

GOLDEN HORN (CHRUSOKERAS)

Latin Quarter

Strategion

1000m

0   200

SEA OF MARMARA (PROPONTIS)

CONSTANTINOPLE

1	Church of Blachernae	12	Column of Arcadius
2	Palace of Blachernae	13	Forum Tauri
3	Monastery of Chora	14	Cistern of the 1001 Columns
4	Monastery of Pammakaris-tos	15	Forum and Column of Constantine
5	Gate of St. Romanus	16	Hippodrome
6	Wall of Theodosius II 413	17	Pharos
7	Golden Gate	18	Church of S.S. Sergius and Bacchus
8	Monastery of Peribleptos	19	Group of palaces
9	Wall of Constantine 330	20	Palace of Bukoleon
10	Church of the Apostle	21	Magnaura
11	Monastery of Pantakrator	22	Hodegethria

23	Hagia Sophia	28	Aqueduct van Valens
24	Pantanassa		
25	Monastery of Magnana		
26	Church of St. Irene		
27	Old Greek Acropolis		

Churches and Monasteries

Cisterns

Wall of ancient Byzantium

Wall of Septimius Severus (c.A.D. 200)

Venetians

Genoese

B

TROY

Roman town.

Troy VI

Troy II

In the hill of Hissarlik near the Hellespont, Schlie-mann during the years following 1870 discovered the city of Troy. Since then others have been digging on this site up to the present time. It now appears that nine layers existed, of which Troy VI precedes Homeric Troy. At that time the city had a Mycenaean civilisation. Schliemann regarded Troy II as the city of Priam. Troy IX is the Roman city which was still in existence at the time of emperor Augustus.

spring

fortress wall Troy VI, (destroyed c.1200 B.C.)

palace

megaron

west gate

south gate

south gate

west gate

fortress wall of Troy II, destroyed (c. 2000 B.C.)

C

80m

0   20

1	Propylaea	11	Stoa of Eumenes II
2	Temple of Nike	12	Theatre of Dionysus
3	Statue of Pallas Athene	13	Odeum of Pericles
4	Parthenon	14	Aqueduct of Pisistratus
5	Erechtheum	15	Temple of Rome and Augustus
6	Porch of the		
7	Wall of Themistocles		
8	Column shafts embedded in wall		
9	Sanctuary of Asclepius		
10	Odeum of Herodes Atticus		

Caryatids

A

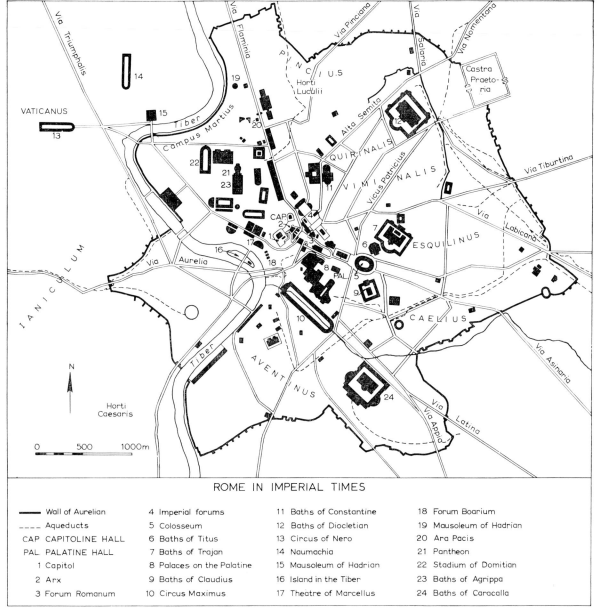

ROME IN IMPERIAL TIMES

⎯⎯ Wall of Aurelian	4 Imperial forums	11 Baths of Constantine	18 Forum Boarium
---- Aqueducts	5 Colosseum	12 Baths of Diocletian	19 Mausoleum of Hadrian
CAP CAPITOLINE HALL	6 Baths of Titus	13 Circus of Nero	20 Ara Pacis
PAL. PALATINE HALL	7 Baths of Trajan	14 Naumachia	21 Pantheon
1 Capitol	8 Palaces on the Palatine	15 Mausoleum of Hadrian	22 Stadium of Domitian
2 Arx	9 Baths of Claudius	16 Island in the Tiber	23 Baths of Agrippa
3 Forum Romanum	10 Circus Maximus	17 Theatre of Marcellus	24 Baths of Caracalla

B

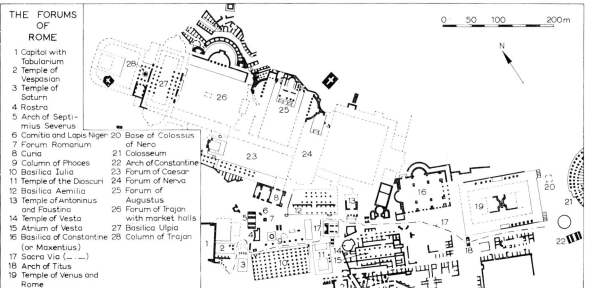

THE FORUMS OF ROME

1 Capitol with Tabularium
2 Temple of Vespasian
3 Temple of Saturn
4 Rostra
5 Arch of Septimius Severus
6 Comitia and Lapis Niger
7 Forum Romanum
8 Curia
9 Column of Phoces
10 Basilica Iulia
11 Temple of the Dioscuri
12 Basilica Aemilia
13 Temple of Antoninus and Faustina
14 Temple of Vesta
15 Atrium of Vesta
16 Basilica of Constantine (or Maxentius)
17 Sacra Via (− . −)
18 Arch of Titus
19 Temple of Venus and Rome
20 Base of Colossus of Nero
21 Colosseum
22 Arch of Constantine
23 Forum of Caesar
24 Forum of Nerva
25 Forum of Augustus
26 Forum of Trajan with market halls
27 Basilica Ulpia
28 Column of Trajan

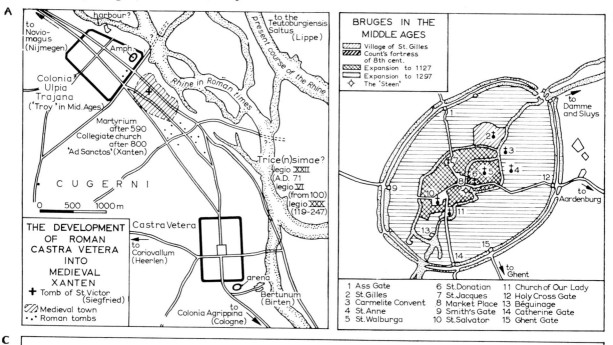

A

to Novio-magus (Nijmegen)

harbour?

Amph.

Colonia Ulpia Trajana ('Troy' in Mid.Ages)

Rhine in Roman times

present course of the Rhine

to the Teutoburgiensis Saltus (Lippe)

Martyrium after 590
Collegiate church after 800
'Ad Sanctos' (Xanten)

C U G E R N I

0   500   1000 m

Trice(n)simae?
legio XXII (A.D. 71)
legio VI (from 100)
legio XXX (119–247)

Castra Vetera

to Coriovallum (Heerlen)

arena

Bertunum (Birten)

to Colonia Agrippina (Cologne)

THE DEVELOPMENT OF ROMAN CASTRA VETERA INTO MEDIEVAL XANTEN
✝ Tomb of St.Victor (Siegfried)
▨ Medieval town
∴ Roman tombs

B

BRUGES IN THE MIDDLE AGES
▧ Village of St. Gilles
▨ Count's fortress of 8th cent.
▦ Expansion to 1127
▢ Expansion to 1297
◇ The 'Steen'

to Damme and Sluys

to Aardenburg

to Ghent

1 Ass Gate
2 St.Gilles
3 Carmelite Convent
4 St.Anne
5 St.Walburga
6 St.Donatian
7 St.Jacques
8 Market Place
9 Smith's Gate
10 St.Salvator
11 Church of Our Lady
12 Holy Cross Gate
13 Béguinage
14 Catherine Gate
15 Ghent Gate

C

THE DEVELOPMENT OF VERSAILLES

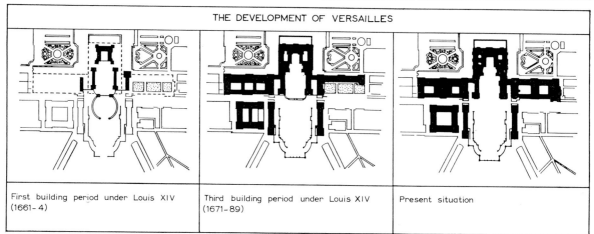

First building period under Louis XIV (1661–4)

Third building period under Louis XIV (1671–89)

Present situation

D

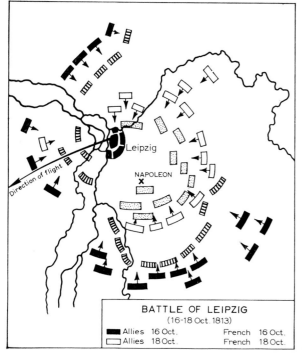

Direction of flight

Leipzig

NAPOLEON
✕

BATTLE OF LEIPZIG
(16-18 Oct. 1813)
◼ Allies 16 Oct.   French 16 Oct.
◻ Allies 18 Oct.   French 18 Oct.

E

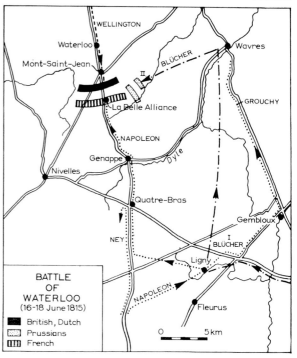

WELLINGTON

Waterloo

Mont-Saint-Jean

BLÜCHER

Wavres

II

GROUCHY

La Belle Alliance

NAPOLEON

Dyle

Genappe

Nivelles

Quatre-Bras

Gembloux

I
BLÜCHER

NEY

Ligny

NAPOLEON

Fleurus

BATTLE OF WATERLOO
(16-18 June 1815)
◼ British, Dutch
▨ Prussians
▥ French

0   5km

A

THE DEVELOPMENT
OF
LONDON

c. 1600
c. 1700
c. 1800

1 Whitehall
2 Downing Street
3 Westminster Abbey
4 Admiralty
5 Guildhall

East India Docks 1806

West India Docks 1802

Surrey Docks 1807

London Docks 1805

London Bridge

Tower

Whitechapel

St Paul's

Hyde Park

Buckingham Palace

Westminster

Greenwich Palace

Thames

B

PARIS AFTER
REBUILDING
BY HAUSSMANN
c. 1865

1 Notre-Dame
2 Louvre
3 Tuileries
4 Hôtel de Ville
5 Pl. de la Concorde
6 Pl. de la République
7 Madeleine
8 Opéra
9 Pl. de l'Étoile
10 Pl. du Trocadéro
11 Mt-Ste-Geneviève
12 Luxembourg
13 Gare St. Lazare
14 Gare de l'Est
15 Gare Montparnasse

Bois de Vincennes

Bois de Boulogne

Seine

C

Montmartre (Mont Marat)

Saint-Denis

Temple

Hôtel de Ville

Notre-Dame

Bastille

Feuillants

Jacobins

Palais-Royal

Louvre

Conciergerie

Cordeliers

Sorbonne

Sainte-Geneviève (Panthéon)

Arsenal

Palais du Luxembourg

Pal Bourbon

Hôtel des Invalides

École Militaire

1 Place de la Concorde
2 Champ de Mars
3 Faubourg St. Antoine

PARIS DURING THE
REVOLUTION c. 1795

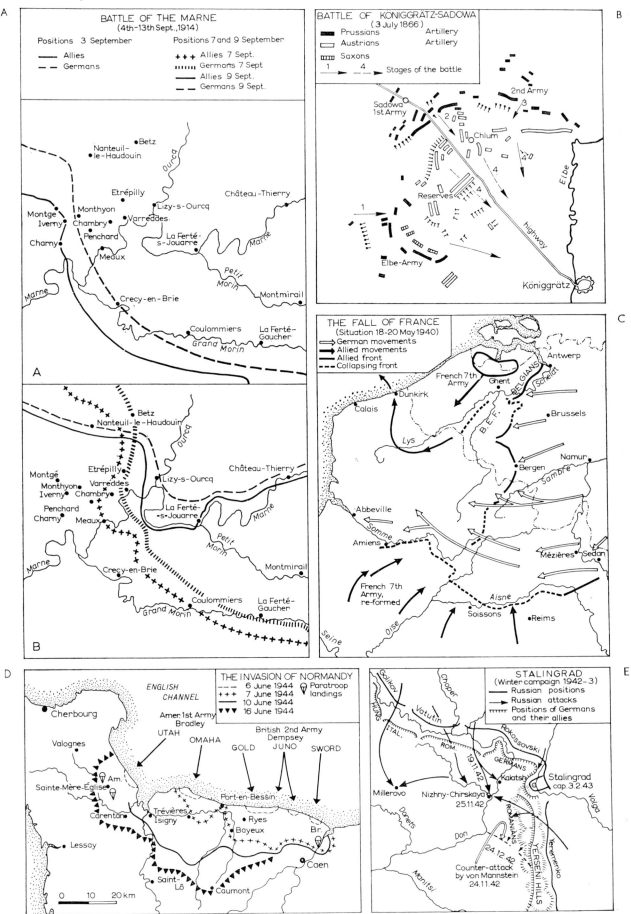

A

BATTLE OF THE MARNE
(4th–13th Sept.,1914)

Positions 3 September

—— Allies
– – – Germans

Positions 7 and 9 September

+ + +   Allies 7 Sept.
ꞮꞮꞮꞮ   Germans 7 Sept.
——   Allies 9 Sept.
– – –   Germans 9 Sept.

B

BATTLE OF KÖNIGGRÄTZ–SADOWA
(3 July 1866)

▬▬ Prussians   Artillery
▭▭ Austrians   Artillery
ꞮꞮꞮꞮ Saxons
1 ——→ 4 —·–·→ Stages of the battle

C

THE FALL OF FRANCE
(Situation 18–20 May 1940)

⇨ German movements
➡ Allied movements
▬ Allied front
▬▬ Collapsing front

D

THE INVASION OF NORMANDY

– – –   6 June 1944
+ + +   7 June 1944
——   10 June 1944
▼▼▼   16 June 1944

⚲ Paratroop landings

E

STALINGRAD
(Winter campaign 1942–3)

——   Russian positions
➡   Russian attacks
ꞮꞮꞮꞮ Positions of Germans and their allies

INDEX TO MAPS

Index to Maps

Figures refer to map numbers. Cross-references are given to names used in different languages or at different periods for places of substantially the same extent and character.